on 3/94

DATE DUE

AN ARTHURIAN DICTIONARY

AN
ARTHURIAN
DICTIONARY

CHARLES & RUTH
MOORMAN

WITH A PREFACE BY
GEOFFREY ASHE

UNIVERSITY PRESS OF MISSISSIPPI

THIS VOLUME IS SPONSORED BY THE

UNIVERSITY OF SOUTHERN MISSISSIPPI

LIBRARY OF CONGRESS CATALOGING IN PUBLICATION DATA

Moorman, Charles.
   An Arthurian dictionary.

   Bibliography: p.
   1. Arthurian romances—Dictionaries. I. Moorman, Ruth, joint author.
II. Title.
PN685.M6   809'.933'51   78–16694
ISBN 0-87805-083-3
ISBN 0-87805-084-1 pbk.

For Wickliffe and Randall

ACKNOWLEDGMENTS

ALTHOUGH IT IS CUSTOMARY in books of this kind to acknowledge by name those friends who have read and commented upon the manuscript, we have decided to refrain from following this practice lest such errors of fact as have inevitably crept into a work as detailed as this be attributed to their, rather than to our, negligence. There are such errors, to be sure, and we should appreciate being informed by readers of those that they find.

We would, however, like to acknowledge the financial aid of the University of Southern Mississippi and its president, Aubrey K. Lucas, and the patience of J. Barney McKee and his staff at the Press.

PREFACE

A REFERENCE BOOK, supposedly, is for looking things up. Of course the supposition is right. Yet a good one is apt to have a further quality. When you consult it on some topic you have in mind, the chances are that your eye will be caught by another item, and then quite likely by another, till you have read more and longer than you intended. I owe much of my education to Brewer's Dictionary of Phrase and Fable, which my parents kept on a shelf within easy reach. Indeed, from merely looking things up in it I soon graduated to reading it, and even taking it on vacations.

Ruth and Charles Moorman have produced a reference book in that noble class. Their Arthurian Dictionary will very properly inform you about King Arthur himself and Sir Lancelot; Merlin and Modred; Tristan and Iseult. But you may well find yourself detained on the way or ensnared afterwards by unlooked-for people and places, or book titles not so often encountered: by Alanus de Insulis, Caerleon, Gaheris, *Libeaus Desconus*, Morgan le Fay, Tribruit, the *Voyage of Bran*. Spell-weaving names, and the spell can work even through an alphabetical list.

The past few years have brought a notable revival of interest in British legend. Medieval story-tellers called this the 'Matter of Britain,' and it was the legend of Arthur and his reign that they meant. Our horizon today is wider, but the hallowed Matter of Britain, richly enlarged beyond its medieval scope, remains at the centre. The Moormans' Dictionary unfolds that realm of imagination as no single reference work has done hitherto.

I value it myself for another reason which is less obvious, yet profoundly important. To run one's eye over the headings, to observe their range and the way some of the topics are presented, is to see the effects of a welcome shift in thinking. This was first remarked on, so far as I know, at the International Arthurian Congress of 1969. It is a movement of convergence. While those who explore the Matter of Britain know it to be immensely complex and variegated, they are seeing it more and more as a whole, and are more and more able to unite many diverse elements in a single scheme.

A generation ago the field was fragmented. The medieval romance-literature was a special study. The early Celtic literature was another. Dark-age British history was another. Dark-age British archaeology (to the meagre extent that it existed) was another. Specialists of different kinds seldom met or engaged in dialogue. Hardly anyone, except a few suspect amateurs, tried to span the gaps or draw all the data into coherence. So the inquirer confronted an 'Arthur of romance,' and an 'Arthur of Welsh legend,' and a nebulous 'historical Arthur,' and sometimes two or three more including even a 'Celtic god Arthur.' These figures were sharply unlike, they did not fit together, and few people—apart from the suspect amateurs—seemed to care much about trying to fit them.

Then the situation began to alter. Several causes combined to modify it. My own belief is that the strongest factor making for a greater Arthurian synthesis was the excavation of South Cadbury Castle in Somerset. Here was an ancient hill-fort, a towering earthwork citadel, long known as 'Camelot' in the lore of the neighbourhood. It could not be the bannered and battlemented Camelot of romance, which was a literary creation. But was it perhaps the headquarters of the historical Arthur, the 'real Camelot' so far as anything could be?

From 1966 to 1970 the Camelot Research Committee carried out excavations. These were directed by Leslie Alcock, who is not only a fine archaeologist but one who takes the fullest account, always, of matters lying outside archaeology ... even legend. The soil and bedrock of Cadbury revealed centuries of occupation, stretching far back into the Iron Age before the Romans. But on the Arthurian issue, local lore was vindicated. The hill to which its mutterings of 'Camelot' had guided the excavators yielded wholly appropriate results. During the period when Arthur might be assumed to have lived, the hill-top had been refortified with a massive defensive system having no parallel anywhere else in Britain. Nothing was found with Arthur's name on it. That is not to be expected in archaeology. But at the very least, the right sort of leader had been in possession at the right time. A vital and unique piece of Arthurian Britain had come to light.

The Cadbury-Camelot project, with the broadcasts and articles that accompanied it, and the books that followed, had two consequences going outside itself. First, it brought together people of different interests. It virtually forced the experts in the various lines—the explorers of legend, the archaeologists, the historians—to talk to each other, to consider each other's work and its bearing on Arthurian problems. The change of mood, I am afraid, remains far from complete. Plenty of archaeologists (for example) would still refuse to allow that their work has any meaning for Arthurian legend, or vice versa. But even here the divorce of one discipline from another can never again be total. Because of Cadbury, and kindred dark-age projects, archaeology has had an impact on Arthurian thinking which no denials can dispel: conspicuously, on views as to which part of Britain was Arthur's home. Here and elsewhere all the special studies remain special, inevitably and rightly. But they overlap and interact; not enough yet, but far more than they used to. In keeping with what has happened, the Moormans' Dictionary draws upon all of them.

The second major effect of Cadbury and its sequels was to give impetus and direction to the aforementioned revival of interest in British legend. It formed a new educated public—not a mass one, but numerous and of high calibre—that now looks beyond the medieval tales and casts a probing gaze on the underlying realities, scanning them from every angle as professional scholars have been learning to do. That process has had its critics. Some say: 'We already have the splendid literature of King Arthur and his knights—what is the point of groping behind it for dark-age "realities" which don't matter anyhow?' Others say:

'If you insist on proving that Arthur was a mud-caked barbarian chief and most of his knights never existed, aren't you spoiling it all?' Not so. The truth is that the quest for roots and the delineation of growth have enriched and deepened the mythos itself. They are not irrelevant, nor do they invalidate.

We indeed have the splendid literature, and its spell survives unbroken in such modern rehandlings as T. H. White's and John Steinbeck's. But lately we have also been witnessing a new creativity inspired by the quest itself, by what it has revealed of the buried facts and the fascination which they too can exert. We have the bestselling dark-age novels of Rosemary Sutcliff and Mary Stewart; John Arden's drama *The Island of the Mighty*; John Heath-Stubbs's heroic poem *Artorius* . . . not to mention a television series based on the reality rather than the legend, *Arthur of the Britons*. And since 1975, we also have academic courses and study-tours, bringing students into contact with this vast realm of legend at all its levels, not solely the medieval.

For the students, for their teachers, and for that active-minded new public, the Dictionary will be a guide without rival. It will supply them with details where old familiarity still needs the reinforcement of knowledge: details about Queen Guinevere and the Round Table and much else. It will give them keys to less eminent figures and to mist-shrouded locations, to Cador and Pellinore, Avalon and Corbenic. It will introduce them to such obscure transmitters of Arthur's fame as Nennius. It will help to align them correctly among the Aedans and Oweins and Rhydderchs of a bewildering antiquity, and among pagan beings even older, known to us through shrines and inscriptions laboriously unearthed. Also, surely, its readers will find hints to lure them towards other regions of legend, history and myth which are not Arthurian, but to which the pursuit of Arthur can lead.

To Ruth and Charles Moorman the thanks of many thousands are due.

Geoffrey Ashe
GLASTONBURY
FEBRUARY, 1978

INTRODUCTION

A BRIEF SURVEY OF THE LITERATURE written in English in every age will bear testimony to the enduring popularity of the legend of King Arthur. Authors of every period have reshaped the story of "that gray king whose name, a ghost,/Streams like a cloud, manshaped, from mountain peak,/And cleaves to cairn and cromlech still" to fit their immediate concerns. In our own time, E. A. Robinson, Charles Williams, and T. H. White among others have written versions of the Arthuriad that mirror twentieth-century man's disillusionment with himself and his alienation from society.

In addition to such large-scale treatments of the story, moreover, there lie buried in the works of hundreds of English authors countless references to the characters and events, both major and minor, of the Arthur saga; the works of Spenser, Milton, the Romantics, the Pre-Raphaelites are full of such allusions and to attempt Yeats' "Cuchulain Comforted" or Book I of *The Fairie Queene* or *The Waste Land* without recourse to their Arthurian backgrounds would be frustrating to say the least and could result in serious misreading.

These poets, moreover, fully expected these allusions to be readily understood by their audiences and so used them to convey their themes and ideas. Since, however, this great body of information is no longer the common possession of even well-educated readers, something of the meaning of these poems is inevitably lost, and the need for some such volume as this one becomes inevitable.

What follows then is a dictionary, a ready reference manual designed for student use, of the characters, places, and topics connected with the legend of King Arthur from its first written appearances through Malory. Like any good dictionary, though, it is meant to serve a variety of students, the graduate student

xiii

who needs a handy list of the twelve battles of Artorius and the undergraduate who is reading *Sir Gawain and the Green Knight* for the first time. Thus here "Gautier de Montbeliard" and "Gawain," like the common "havoc" and the exotic "haversine" in the *Random House Dictionary*, lie cheek by jowl. Even so, it attempts neither to be complete in its listing nor comprehensive in its discussions; it includes, for example, for the most part only Celtic, French, German, and English materials. It certainly does not intend in controversial matters to be authoritative. On matters of contention (and in Arthurian studies they are both minute and legion) we have followed standard authorities, e.g., R. S. Loomis on Celtic problems. Entries are generally limited to characters and places which either appear in more than one work or are important to the legend. The student who hopes to find in it a complete discussion of the various theories of the historicity of Arthur will be disappointed; the student who comes to it in order to identify a reference in Tennyson or T. S. Eliot will be more than satisfied. It is, in a sense, a "shorter" Arthurian dictionary for which the "longer" version does not exist.

Since, however, the dictionary form, despite its virtues, does not allow for a unified presentation of the whole legend, a sketch of its development here may prove useful. For while we have a plenitude of chronicles and romances dealing with the great British hero and his court there is no one poem or history, and thus no single entry, which brings together all the themes and motifs of the tradition.

One major factor which must also be considered in dealing with the development of the Arthur story is that upon emerging from the oral tradition it takes the form of two sharply distinguishable literary forms. Our information concerning the historicity of Arthur and the origins of the tales concerning him comes basically from two types of sources: the works of chroniclers, whom we would call historians, and the body of Celtic folklore that has come down to us. The first evidences are thus both historical and mythological.

Most modern students agree that there was indeed a historical Arthur, though there was never a King Arthur of the type celebrated in the later legends. The Arthur from which the legend grew may well have been a military leader of the Britons in their wars against Saxon invaders during the late fifth century. The most contemporaneous account of the period, however, the monk Gildas's *De Excidio et Conquestu Britanniae*, written in about 540, does not mention Arthur, although it does describe the battle of Mount Badon, later to be associated with Arthur. The name *Arthur* first appears in a Welsh poem, *Gododdin*, written presumably by the poet Aneirin early in the seventh century. An elegy for the British who fell in the northern battles against the Angles, the poem says of one hero, though the line may be an interpolation, that he "glutted black ravens on the rampart of the fort, though he was not Arthur," that he fed the ravens with dead bodies, though not to the extent that Arthur had. The importance of this single allusion is that it demonstrates that in not much more than a hundred years after Mount Badon, Arthur had achieved something like legendary status.

The first account of Arthur by a historian, however, is given in the *Historia Britonum* written about 800 by the Welsh priest Nennius, although there exists a possibility, first indicated by N. K. Chadwick, that Nennius confuses the hero of Badon with a Galloway prince, Arthur of Dalriada, who fought the Saxons in the North and who may be the Arthur celebrated by Aneirin and the Welsh bard, Taliesin. Nennius relates fully the coming of the Saxons and the first years of Saxon victories; eventually he describes how one Arthur, who fought "along with the kings of the Britons, but was himself a leader of the wars" (*cum regibus Brittonum, sed ipse erat dux bellorum*), fought twelve victorious battles, apparently throughout England, against Octa, the son of Hengist, culminating in the victory at Mount Badon, where Arthur alone slew 960 of the enemy.

The term *dux bellorum* is something of a mystery. It may indicate simply that Arthur was a commander of British forces or that he was a member of a Roman family who had successfully organized and maintained a kind of mobile cavalry troop which could effectively combat the Saxon infantry. Whatever his rank, however—and whatever it is, it is not that of king—his importance as the savior of the British is clear.

Something of the aura of legend that had come to surround the native hero in the three-hundred-odd years since the battle of Mount Badon can be seen in Nennius's accounts of the number of Saxons he killed and of two miracles concerning him. These two miracles, set down in a section of Nennius's work called *De Mirabilibus Britanniae*, recount how a heap of stones in south Wales is topped by a stone bearing the footprint of Arthur's dog, Cabal, which though moved always returns to its place, and how the grave of Arthur's son Anir varies in length each time it is measured.

The *Annales Cambriae*, or *Annals of Wales*, which were probably gathered together in the early tenth century but which may be very nearly contemporaneous with the events they record, contain two allusions to Arthur. The first, dating the battle of Mount Badon at 516, asserts that at that battle Arthur bore the "cross of our Lord Jesus Christ on his shoulders [probably his shield] three days and three nights."

The second of the two statements in the *Annales Cambriae* is of greater importance to the legend. In 537, we are told, occurred the "battle of Camlann, in which Arthur and Medrawt fell." There can be little doubt that Medrawt is the Modred of later legend, that the story as we know it is already beginning to take shape, and that it was from the beginning given a tragic ending.

Although other early chronicles furnish us with bits and pieces of the growing tradition of Arthur's greatness, it is with Geoffrey of Monmouth that we have the real beginning of Arthurian literature, for in his *Historia Regum Britanniae* is found for the first time the skeleton of the whole legend of Arthur to which previous chronicles had only alluded. We have the familiar story of Arthur's birth—how Uther falls in love with Igerna, wife of the Duke of Cornwall, and how through a substitution instituted by

Merlin, Uther is accepted by Igerna as her husband and bears Arthur. On coming to the throne at age fifteen Arthur conquers not only the Saxons but the neighboring kings as well and, after a period of peace, most of Europe. He marries Guinevere and establishes a great medieval court. Then challenged by the authority of Rome, the great king embarks upon a second European expedition, leaving his kingdom under the regency of his queen and his nephew, Modred. Word comes to him en route that his regents have betrayed him, and he turns back to England. There he defeats Modred in a series of battles during the last of which he himself is apparently mortally wounded but is carried to the Isle of Avalon to be healed.

However, Geoffrey's contribution to the Arthurian tradition lies in more than his setting down for the first time a coherent account of the mass of legend which presumably had been accumulating for six hundred years, ever since the battle of Camlann. Geoffrey also places the legend in the setting it is to assume from his time onward. Arthur is no mere elected cavalry leader but a great king presiding over a chivalric court so magnificent that all the courts of Europe copy its manner and dress. His enemies are no longer bands of Germanic invaders but the kings of Europe and even the Emperor of Rome himself. Arthur's knights are products of the new chivalry whose deeds on the battlefield and in tournaments and whose behavior at court are inspired and refined by the hope of finding favor in their ladies' eyes.

One of the first and most influential works based on Geoffrey's *Historia* was the *Roman de Brut*, or *Story of Brutus*, the mythical founder of Britain, by the Norman poet Wace, a work which is in the main a French verse paraphrase of Geoffrey's Latin prose. Written in 1155, Wace's *Brut* was apparently composed for Eleanor of Aquitaine, whose husband, Henry II of England, had assumed the throne the year before, to supply that noble lady with some knowledge of the nation over which she was to rule. Although it follows Geoffrey closely, Wace's lively poem omits some details—particularly Merlin's prophecies—and adds some new material. He emphasizes, as would be expected of a court poet, the courtly elements of the tale, especially the chivalric figure of Gawain; accounts for the creation of the Round Table, at which all might sit equally; discusses the habits of the *conteurs*, or storytellers; and enlarges on Geoffrey's descriptions of banquets and festival occasions.

The Arthurian chronicle tradition did not, however, end with Wace, for Wace's *Brut* in turn became the source of the first English metrical chronicle, Layamon's *Brut*. Just as Wace's *Brut* reflected the chivalric courtly tradition, so Layamon's poem is close in spirit and method to the Anglo-Saxon heroic tradition. Layamon's chief expansions of his source are found in his descriptions of battles, just as those of Wace appear in his descriptions of life at court. Layamon is, wherever possible, dramatic and graphic, particularly in the use of direct discourse and figurative speech. Arthur himself is seen as a rough warlord, not a courtly gentleman. Layamon's additions are also important to the development of the legend. Fairies are present at Arthur's birth to bestow gifts on him; the Round Table is founded not as in Wace, simply as a means of bestowing equality of station on Arthur's knights, but because a brawl makes necessary such a device. Arthur dreams before his return to Britain of the doom that lies before him and at the end he announces to Constantine, his successor, that he will indeed return to help the British.

With Layamon the early chronicle tradition of Arthur comes to an end. Traced from its spare and illusive beginnings, it manifests a consistent pattern of development in which the major concern is historical. The chroniclers are writing what is to them the history of Britain, a history made up of all sorts of what seem to us to be extraneous elements, but always aimed at presenting the Arthur story within the context of the growth of the British nation. Thus Geoffrey, Wace, and Layamon present the whole story of Arthur from his birth through his tragic defeat and miraculous departure to Avalon. They are not concerned with particular episodes of the legend for their own sakes nor with the adventures, however marvelous, of individual knights. For this kind of story we must turn to the tradition of Arthurian romance.

The Arthurian tradition in romance, properly speaking, begins with Chrétien de Troyes, the first writer of romances. Its roots, however, lie so deeply embedded in Celtic folktales, both oral and written, that some knowledge of these early tales is necessary to an understanding of the tradition in which Chrétien is working.

It seems certain, first of all, that the romance tradition does not evolve from that of the chronicles but that both go back to a common body of Arthurian legends which grew slowly among the Welsh during the centuries following their expulsion from Britain by the Saxon invaders. This body of legends is composed of at least two elements, a fact which accounts for our being able to distinguish between a chronicle strain and a romance strain in the development of the Arthur story.

There was, as one would expect, a glorification of the deeds of the historical warrior, a magnification of the *dux bellorum* of Mount Badon into a great king whose conquests encompassed nearly all of Europe and who numbered among his followers the greatest knights the world has ever seen. But as we have noted, in this process of development from history into heroic literature, another element, mythology, often influences and in fact becomes so entangled with the facts of history that myth and history are well-nigh inseparable. It is not surprising, therefore, that the Arthur story came to incorporate many of the incidents and characters of older Celtic myth and legend. For example, both the names and attributes of Sir Gawain and Sir Lancelot have been traced to Celtic sun gods, and the bridge from which Gawain falls in Chrétien's *The Knight of the Cart* is probably descended from numerous references in Celtic mythology to crossings into the "Otherworld."

It is with the romances of Chrétien de Troyes that the Arthurian romance tradition properly begins. Although a number of Chrétien's poems and translations have been lost, five, possibly six, have come down to us: *Erec and Enide*; *Cligès*; *Lancelot*; *Yvain*, or *The Knight of the Lion*; *Perceval*, or *The Story of the Grail*; and perhaps *William of England*. The first five are parts of the so-called Matter of Britain, that subject division of the medieval romance which contains the Arthur stories and deals with the adventures of individual round table knights. *Erec and Enide*, for example, tells of the courtship, marriage, and marital troubles of one Erec, son of Lac. The romance begins "in Spring, at Easter" at the court of King Arthur in Cardigan. Erec, having undertaken the quest of the White Hart—a typical beginning to such a story—fights a joust on behalf of Enide, the daughter of a poor vavasour, and brings her to Arthur's court to be his bride. However, once married, he neglects to keep up his reputation in arms and upon discovering from Enide that he is generally thought to be uxorious sets out on a series of adventures to regain his reputation. These adventures comprise the greater part of *Erec and Enide*, and though they appear at first sight to be rambling and digressive, they actually form a pattern in which Erec can be seen to regain, step by step, his self-confidence and reputation. Following his trials he returns briefly to Arthur's court before going on to claim his own throne upon the death of his father.

It will be seen that in *Erec and Enide*, Chrétien is not in the least interested, as were the chroniclers, in presenting a history of the rise and fall of Arthur's kingdom. His major purpose is to present a series of adventures, very loosely bound together, involving a particular hero of Arthur's court. The court itself is simply a point of departure from which the knight sets forth, and its main function seems to be to set the scene of the story in Logres, Arthurland, and to assure us of the hero's worth by assigning him a place at the Round Table.

In time the Arthurian romance spread well beyond France. There are extant romances dealing with Arthur's heroes in

Spain, Portugal, Italy, Germany, Holland, the Scandinavian countries and, of course, England. Like Chrétien later romancers made little or no attempt to view their material from any sort of historical perspective, to see the rise, flowering, and downfall of a civilization. To tell an entertaining story was their principal aim. Later writers, as we shall see, were to incorporate the romance material into the framework of the chronicle story; but before we can properly deal with them, we must examine one group of Arthurian romances which because of its independent origin and development must be set off from the general stream of the romance—that dealing with the adventures of the knights of the Holy Grail.

The origins of the Holy Grail legend are very difficult to ascertain, and indeed Arthurian specialists differ more widely here than on any other matter. The Grail first appears in the last of the romances of Chrétien, *Perceval*, or the *Conte del Graal*, in which, as in *Lancelot*, Chrétien professes simply to be working with material given to him by a patron, Philip of Flanders. The *Conte del Graal* deals for the most part with the adventures of the youthful Perceval, who leaves his widowed mother to enter training at Arthur's court. In the course of an early adventure Perceval encounters two men fishing, one of whom directs him to a nearby castle for shelter. There he finds a man lying on a couch. A strange procession enters carrying a bleeding lance, two ten-branched candlesticks, a *graal* (a large dish), and a silver carving plate. This same *graal* accompanies each course of the meal that follows. Perceval, remembering the advice of a tutor, refrains from inquiring about what he sees, sleeps, and wakes to find the castle deserted. Later he learns that had he asked the meaning of what he saw, the maimed Fisher King, who had directed him to the castle, would have been healed.

From this strange and illusory tale stems the Grail branch of Arthurian romance. One of the first "continuators" of Chrétien, Robert de Boron, provides us with the mythological antecedents of the *graal* which occupies such an important place in Chrétien's *Conte del Graal.* This vessel, says Robert, is none other than the Holy Grail itself, the vessel which was first used by Christ at the Last Supper and later to catch the blood flowing from his wounds. After the crucifixion the Grail was given by Pilate to Joseph of Arimathea, who was instructed by Christ in a vision to form a companionship to guard the holy chalice. After a series of great trials Bron, Joseph's brother-in-law, called the Rich Fisher, carried the Grail westward, presumably to Glastonbury in England, leaving Joseph to die in his own land.

It is not certain, of course, that Robert's *Joseph d'Arimathie* derives directly from Chrétien's *Conte del Graal*; both writers may be working independently from lost sources. Yet certain correspondences suggest that both poems indeed concern the same subject; and Robert, writing perhaps ten years after Chrétien, clearly identifies Chrétien's *graal* with the most sacred of all Christian relics.

The casual reader may therefore be surprised to learn that heated controversy has raged over the source and origin of the vessel. The main reasons for the argument are that Chrétien's narrative is unfinished and that its *graal* references are vague and mysterious, perhaps deliberately so. Three principal theories of origin, as well as a number of lesser conjectures, have arisen concerning the source of the Grail legend.

There are, as one would expect, a number of scholars who maintain that the Grail was *ab origine* a part of the Christian legend which Chrétien inherited and to which he added the character of the Grail knight and the conception of the quest. According to this theory, the procession at the mysterious castle is a Eucharistic procession, much like that used in Byzantine ceremonies, and the lance is that with which the centurion Longinus pierced the side of our Lord. Others have suggested that the Grail and lance were sexual symbols which were originally part of the initiation rites of a mystery religion, part Christian, part pagan. Celticists see in the Grail vestiges of Celtic myth and have observed a number of parallels between Bron, the Fisher King, and King Bran of Welsh legend and traced the various articles of the Grail procession to Celtic prototypes.

Whatever its origins, however, the Grail enters the main stream of Arthurian literature as a Christian symbol, and from Chrétien onward the quest of the Holy Grail rapidly develops into a distinct branch of Arthurian tradition.

Three streams, then, fed the great river of the fully developed story of the rise and fall of Arthurian chivalry: the early histories of the chroniclers, the chivalric romances of the Matter of Britain, and the legend of the Holy Grail. For hundreds of years each ran its own way, concerned only with its own themes and devices and touching the others only in occasional references to Arthur's court, the traditional starting point of chivalric adventures. At length, after preliminary attempts by the authors of the thirteenth-century Old French Vulgate Cycle to combine and to unify these facets of the legend, they found their resolution in Sir Thomas Malory's *Morte Darthur*, a work which, although removed by centuries from the oral tradition, pulls together the scattered threads of meaning inherent in the early works and weaves the story's definitive garment.

To return to the dictionary, explanations of the very brief bibliography and of the dictionary forms seem in order. Since full Arthurian bibliographies are readily available in public and university libraries, it seems pointless simply to reprint here the titles of easily accessible items, thus increasing the cost of the dictionary. Only those general commentaries, all of which are standard authorities, that served as major sources for this volume and to which the student may turn both for further information and for more specialized bibliography are cited. Editions of individual works, though frequently consulted, are in the interest of brevity not listed. Arthurian scholars are usually scrupulous in acknowledging their fellow workers, and the student will find himself quickly drawn from these general accounts into specialized discussions.

Those names capitalized within the entries are themselves entries, and although titles are italicized but not capitalized, they are for the most part also entries. Spellings, systems of numbering, etc., are generally those of R. S. Loomis: *Arthurian Literature in the Middle Ages.* The numbering of the Triads is that of Rachel Bromwich.

BIBLIOGRAPHY

I. General Works

Ackerman, R. W. *An Index of the Arthurian Names in Middle English.* Stanford, 1952.

Bruce, James Douglas. *The Evolution of Arthurian Romance from the Beginnings Down to the Year 1300.* Baltimore, 1923, reissued Gloucester, Mass., 1958.

Chambers, E. K. *Arthur of Britain.* London, 1927, reissued Cambridge, 1964.

Lewis, C. B. *Classical Mythology and Arthurian Romance.* London, 1932.

Loomis, R. S. (ed.). *Arthurian Literature in the Middle Ages.* Oxford, 1959.

Loomis, R. S. *The Development of Arthurian Romance.* London, 1963.

Parry, John J., and Margaret Schlauch. *Arthurian Bibliography.* Vol. I (1922–1929), Vol. II (1930–1935). New York. Subsequent yearly bibliographies are published in *Modern Language Quarterly* (1940–1963) and in the *Bibliographical Bulletin of the International Arthurian Society* (1949–   ).

West, G. D. *An Index of Proper Names in French Arthurian Verse Romances, 1300–1500.* Toronto, 1969.

West, G. D. *An Index of Proper Names in French Arthurian Prose Romances.* Toronto, 1978.

II. The Celtic Tradition

Bromwich, Rachel (ed.). *Trioedd Ynys Prydein: The Welsh Triads.* Cardiff, 1961.

Loomis, R. S. *Arthurian Tradition and Chrétien de Troyes.* New York, 1949.

Loomis, R. S. *Celtic Myth and Arthurian Romance.* New York, 1927.

Loomis, R. S. *Wales and the Arthurian Legend.* Cardiff, 1956.

III. The Chronicle Materials

Alcock, Leslie. *Arthur's Britain.* London, 1971.

Barber, Richard. *The Figure of Arthur.* London, 1972.

Fletcher, R. A. *The Arthurian Material in the Chronicles.* Cambridge, Mass., 1906.

Tatlock, J. S. P. *The Legendary History of Britain.* Los Angeles, 1950.

XXV

IV. The Romances

Cross, Tom Peete, and William Albert Nitze. *Lancelot and Guenevere*, Chicago, 1930.

Hibbard, Laura A. *Medieval Romance in England*. New York, 1924.

Holmes, Urban Tigner, Jr. *A History of Old French Literature*. Chapel Hill, 1937.

Stevens, John. *Medieval Romance*. London, 1973.

Taylor, A. B. *An Introduction to Medieval Romance*. New York, 1930.

V. The Tristan Story

Eisner, Sigmund. *The Tristan Legend: A Study in Sources*. Evanston, Ill., 1969.

Loomis, Gertrude Schoepperle. *Tristan and Isolt: A Study of the Sources of the Romance*. Frankfurt, 1913.

VI. The Holy Grail

Brown, Arthur C. L. *The Origin of the Grail Legend*. Cambridge, Mass., 1943.

Holmes, Urban T., Jr. and Sister M. Amelia Klenke. *Chrétien de Troyes and the Grail*. Chapel Hill, 1959.

Loomis, R. S. *The Grail: From Celtic Myth to Christian Symbol*. New York, 1963.

Sacker, Hugh. *An Introduction to Wolfram's Parzival*. Cambridge, 1963.

Weston, Jessie L. *The Quest of the Holy Grail*. London, 1913.

Weston, Jessie L. *From Ritual to Romance*. Cambridge, 1920.

VII. Malory

Bennett, J. A. W. (ed.). *Essays on Malory*. Oxford, 1968.

Lumiansky, R. M. (ed.). *Malory's Originality*. Baltimore, 1964.

Vinaver, Eugene. *Malory*. Oxford, 1929.

AN ARTHURIAN DICTIONARY

A

Aballach (Avallach, Avalloc). See also AVALON. In the Welsh TRIAD 70, the father of the goddess (?) MODRON, who in later legends may become MORGAN LE FAY.

Aberteivi. Present day Welsh name for CARDIGAN.

Accalon. Appears in the later portion of the PSEUDO-ROBERT *Merlin* continuation. In MALORY he is the paramour of MORGAN LE FAY and is slain by ARTHUR.

Acheflour. Heroine of *Sir Perceval of Galles*. Her name is a corruption of BLANCHEFLOR.

Acts of St. Simon and St. Jude. Apocryphal scripture possibly used by the author of the *Estoire del Saint Graal* to supply more detail for the period between JOSEPH and ARTHUR.

Adam de la Halle (c. 1245–c. 1288). Thirteenth-century French lyric poet and dramatist. He notes that MORGAN LE FAY had as a lover Hellekin, a fairy prince, and his *Jeu de la Feuillée* (1262) contains references to imitation *tables rondes*.

Adam of Domerham. Monk at the abbey of GLASTONBURY who in his history of the abbey (c. 1291) records the abbey tradition that ARTHUR's tomb was discovered in 1190 or 1191. He states that the abbot ordered the site to be surrounded by curtains before the digging began.

Ade. Niece of the lord of the Castle LIMORS who saves LANCELOT and becomes his mistress in *Lanzelet*.

Adomnan. Abbot (?) of Hy (c. 700) who wrote a life of ST. COLUMBA in which there is mention of an "Artuir" as one of the three sons of KING AEDAN. According to this account, ST. COLUMBA prophesied ARTUIR's death in battle, and he does indeed die in a battle with the Miathi, after which his brother, ECHOID BUIDE, succeeded their father as king.

Adonis, Cult of. Pagan cult thought by Jessie L. Weston (*From*

Ritual to Romance) to have been widely diffused throughout medieval Europe and to be the source of the GRAIL romances. In the initiatory rite of the cult, a dish and a lance resembling those described in CHRÉTIEN's *Perceval* were used.

Adventures of Art, Son of Conn. An ancient Irish ECHTRA recounting the visitation of a mortal to the household of a god and thought to contain parallels to PERCEVAL's visit to the GRAIL castle.

Adventures of Cormac. An ancient Irish ECHTRA thought to contain parallels to CHRÉTIEN's *Conte del Graal*.

Adventures of the Sons of Eochaid Mugmedon. An ancient Irish ECHTRA containing an analogue of the LOATHLY LADY TRANSFORMED motif.

Adventurous Palace. In the Vulgate *Lancelot* BORS, after seeing the GRAIL, spends two nights here. Later PELLES has the mad LANCELOT bound and brought here to be cured by the GRAIL.

Aedan Mac Gabrain. King of DALRIADA in the late sixth century. In ADOMNAN's life of ST. COLUMBA he has three sons, one of whom is ARTUIR. In the *Annals of Tigernach* ARTUR is one of AEDAN's sons, but in the list of Pictish kings he is his grandson. In *Cuchulain's Sick Bed* he is the father of Fanh, the fairy who loves CUCHULAIN.

Afallenau (Apple Trees). An anonymous twelfth-century Welsh poetic fragment contained in the BLACK BOOK OF CARMARTHEN. It contains possibly the oldest reference to MERLIN, here MYRDDIN, a madman living in the CALEDONIAN FOREST.

Aglaval (Agglovale, Aglarale). PERCEVAL's brother, father of Moriaen in *Moriaen*, a fourteenth-century Dutch verse romance. He plays a considerable part in the Vulgate *Lancelot* and in MALORY: he is slain by LANCELOT in the abduction of GUINEVERE.

Agned, Mount. The site of Arthur's eleventh battle listed by NENNIUS.

Agravain (Engre Vains). One of GAWAIN's brothers in the VUL-
GATE CYCLE and in MALORY. He joins MODRED in plot-
ting against ARTHUR and is killed by LANCELOT.

Aigidecht Arthūir (The Entertainment of Arthur). Lost Irish
saga listed in the twelfth-century *Book of Leinster*.

Ailred of Rievaulx. A Yorkshire monk who in his *Speculum
Caritatis* (1141–42) notes that a novice once wept over
the tales of ARTHUR.

Airem. High King of Ireland, considered by some as an Irish
counterpart of ARTHUR.

Alain le Gros. The father of PERCEVAL in ROBERT DE BORON's
Joseph and *Merlin*, in *Perlesvaus*, and in the *Didot Perceval*.
In the Vulgate *Estoire del Saint Graal*, he is the first of
the FISHER KINGS and builds the Castle of CORBENIC. The
second keeper of the GRAIL, he on one occasion feeds
a multitude with a single fish.

Alanus de Insulis (1114–1203). At one time thought to be the
author of a notable set of twelfth-century commentaries
on the *Prophetiae Merlini* of GEOFFREY OF MONMOUTH.
He is also called Alan (or Alain) of Lille, and may have
been Alan, the Prior of Tewkesbury.

Albion. Ancient name of Britain among the Greeks and Romans. The name is perhaps Celtic, but was understood
by the Romans to have come from the Latin *albus* for
"white," a reference to the cliffs of Dover.

Albrecht von Scharfenberg. Thirteenth-century imitator in his
Seifrid de Ardemont and *Jüngerer Titurel* of WOLFRAM's
Parzival.

Alexander, Bishop of Lincoln (d. 1148). The ecclesiastical superior of GEOFFREY OF MONMOUTH who (c. 1132) urged
him to lay aside the *Historia Regum Britanniae* in order to
write the *Prophetiae Merlini*.

Alexander the Great (356–323 B.C.). Along with ARTHUR and
Charlemagne one of the great heroes of the romances
whose legendary deeds may have inspired the early
Arthurian writers. The mysterious circumstances of

ARTHUR's birth, his worldwide conquests, and even the GRAIL quest, this latter in the hero's journey to the Earthly Paradise and the castle of the sun, all have parallels in the Alexander Story.

Alexandre. Father of CLIGÈS in CHRÉTIEN's *Cligès*. He is the elder son of the Emperor of Constantinople.

Alfred of Beverley (fl. 1140). A twelfth-century English chronicler who abridged GEOFFREY OF MONMOUTH's *Historia* (c. 1149).

Alis. Brother of CLIGÈS in CHRÉTIEN's *Cligès*.

Alixandre L'Orphelin. A section of the *Prophécies de Merlin* named after Alexander, who is a nephew of KING MARK. The title is also that of a French romantic history inserted into a late prose *Tristan* and used by MALORY. Alixandre is the son of BODWYN of Wales, the husband of Alys le Beale Pylgrym, and the victim of KING MARK.

Almesbury (Amesbury). Town in Wiltshire where MALORY's GUINEVERE retires to a nunnery after ARTHUR's passing.

Alphasem. In the Vulgate *Estoire del Saint Graal* the ruler of Terre Foraine who builds a castle for the GRAIL.

Amadís de Gaula. Fourteenth-century Spanish romance, perhaps translated from Portuguese, the central plot of which coincides with that of the LANCELOT story. Like LANCELOT, Amadís falls in love with his sovereign's wife, Oriana, saves her from an abductor, and is the victim of her jealousy. Many incidents, particularly the assignations, in one of which Amadís grasps Oriana's hands through a grating, are also very similar. This Spanish Arthurian imitation is unique in Spain in that, unlike the typical Spanish romance of the period, it extols strongly the chivalric virtues of love and honor.

Ambrosius Aurelianus. In NENNIUS and in GILDAS the survivor of a noble Roman family who leads the Britons against Anglo-Saxon invaders after the withdrawal of the Roman legions and who is also a wonder-worker. GEOFFREY combined his miraculous exploits with those of the

Welsh MYRDDIN to produce MERLIN, whom he identifies with Ambrosius, EMRYS WLEDIG in the Welsh tradition. The British leader he retained as Aurelius Ambrosius. Cf. VORTIGERN.

Andret (Audret). Nephew of MARK, who hates TRISTAN and plots to ruin him and ISEULT in THOMAS.

Andreas Capellanus. Once thought to have been chaplain to MARIE DE CHAMPAGNE, though his identity is now regarded as uncertain. His *De Amore* is one of the sources of our knowledge of the customs of Courtly Love.

Andrew of Wyntown. Author of *Orygnale Cronykil of Scotland* (c. 1425) which attributes to Huchown "the great *Gest off Arthure* and the *Awntyre off Gàwane.*"

Aneirin. One of the late sixth-century poets to whom the Welsh elegy *Gododdin* is attributed.

Anfortas. In WOLFRAM'S *Parzival* and in Wagner's *Parsifal* (as Amfortas), PERCEVAL'S maternal uncle, keeper of the GRAIL at the GRAIL castle. When PERCEVAL visits there, Anfortas gives him a precious sword.

Angharat Law Eurawc (Angharad Golden-Hand). In *Peredur* a maiden at ARTHUR'S court whom PEREDUR loves and to whom he swears an oath of silence to Christians until she pledges her love to him.

Anglesey (Mona). Island off the north coast of Wales separated from the mainland by the Menai Straits. In the BLACK BOOK OF CARMARTHEN, Poem XXXI, "Cai the Fair went to ANGLESEY [Môn] to destroy hosts [or 'lions'?]. His shield was a fragment [or 'polished'?] against Palug's Cat." GAWAIN passes the island in *Sir Gawain and the Green Knight* on his journey.

Anglides. Mother of ALIXANDRE L'ORPHELIN.

Anguysh (Agwysshe). King of Ireland and father of ISEULT.

Anir (Amr). ARTHUR'S son whose grave was one of two marvels associated with ARTHUR described by NENNIUS. Cf. LLACHEU and LOHOOT.

Anjou. Old province in France, now part of the departments of Maine-et-Loire, Indre-et-Loire, and Sarthe and Mayenne. It has been equated with "Anschowe" in WOLFRAM's *Parzival.* The GRAIL kings and PERCEVAL's father are Angevins.

Anna. Sister of ARTHUR (according to GEOFFREY, WACE, et al.), wife of LOT of Lothian (GEOFFREY), of LLEW AP KYNVARCH (Welsh versions), and mother of GAWAIN. Cf. MORGAUSE.

Annales Cambriae. Tenth-century chronicle compiled in Wales. Under the year 516 it lists the Battle of BADON in which ARTHUR and the Britons were victorious and under 537 the Battle of CAMLANN in which ARTHUR and MEDRAWT were killed.

Annals of Tigernach. Irish manuscript dated 1088. In contradiction to ADOMNAN this document lists for the year after the death of ST. COLUMBA the death of ARTHUR and three other sons of AEDAN in the Battle of Circhind.

Annwfn (Annwn). The Celtic "Otherworld," sometimes an island, sometimes an underworld kingdom. In *The Spoils of Annwfn (Preiddeu Annwfn)* ARTHUR led an expedition to Annwfn. PWYLL is Lord of Annwfn in the FIRST BRANCH of the *Mabinogion.*

Anoeth. Along with Caer Oeth, appears in the *Verses on the Graves,* in TRIAD 52, "Three Exalted Prisoners of the Island of Britain," and in *Culhwch and Olwen.* In the latter two ARTHUR is connected with this "castle of great wonders." In the *Verses on the Graves* "anoeth" appears in the controversial line "the world's wonder [or difficulty] a grave for ARTHUR." Cf. CAER OETH AND ANOETH.

Antoine, Maistre. One of MERLIN's scribes in *Prophécies de Merlin.*

Antor (Auctor). ARTHUR's foster father to whom MERLIN entrusts him in ROBERT's *Merlin* and the Vulgate *Estoire de Merlin.* Cf. ECTOR.

Anwas (The Winged). A warrior of CULHWCH's listed in the BLACK BOOK OF CARMARTHEN and in *Culhwch and Olwen.*

Apollo. TRISTAN's uncle in the prose *Tristan*.

Apollonius of Tyre. Anonymous romance popular in the Middle Ages, the oldest extant version of which is in Latin (5th– 6th century A.D.). The legend of the floating coffin of the hero's wife appears again in *Mort Artu*.

Aquitaine. A Roman province (*Aquitania*) stretching from the Pyrenees to the Garonne. It became part of France in 1137 through the marriage of ELEANOR OF AQUITAINE to Louis VII, then passed to the English kings through her marriage in 1152 to Henry of Anjou, who became HENRY II of England in 1154.

Araby, Mount of. Where in the *Morte Arthure* and in MALORY ARTHUR kills the giant RITHO. The place may be Mt. Snowdon in Wales. Cf. MONT-SAINT-MICHEL.

Arawn. Hunter and king of the Celtic "Otherworld" in the first branch of the *Mabinogion*. He exchanges places with PWYLL for a year.

Arfderydd (Arderydd). Identified with ARTHURET in Liddesdale, about eight miles north of CARLISLE. The Battle of Arfderydd (dated 573 in the *Annales Cambriae*) is listed in Welsh TRIAD 84 as one of "The Three Futile Battles of the Island of Britain" in which RHYDDERCH (?) defeated GWENDDOLAU. One manuscript of the *Annales Cambriae*, however, states that at Arfderydd the sons of Eliffer defeated GWENDDOLAU and that MYRDDIN there went mad.

Argante. The queen who will cure ARTHUR's wounds in AVALON in LAYAMON's *Brut*. The name may be a corruption of MORGAN (Morgant).

Argyll. Present-day name for that part of DALRIADA ruled by AEDAN MAC GABRAIN.

Armes Prydein (The Prophecy of Britain). Welsh poem (c. 930) prophesying the coming of CADWALADR and CYNAN to recover the land lost to the Saxons.

Armorica. Latin name of BRITTANY or Lesser Britain.

Arnaut, Daniel (fl. 1180–1210). Provençal poet attached to the court of Richard I of England. A probably mistaken statement by Tasso credits him with a prose *Lancelot*.

Arnaut-Guillem de Marsan (fl. 1160–70). Nobleman from Gascony who wrote *Ensenhamen del Cavalher* in which he recommends Arthurian heroes along with Paris, Aeneas, and Apollonius as models of behavior.

L'Art D'Amors. Translation of Ovid's *Ars Amandi* listed by CHRÉTIEN in *Cligès* as one of his works.

Arthour and Merlin. Late thirteenth-century English romance in rimed couplets expanded from the chronicles and the VULGATE sequel.

Arthur. A 642-line English poem of the late fourteenth century written in four-stress rimed couplets. It recounts only the birth of ARTHUR, his battle with the Giant of MONT-SAINT-MICHEL, and the last battle.

Arthur, King. Generally believed to have been of Roman descent or a Romanized Celt of the late fifth century and early sixth, although some critics believe him to be of Irish extraction. The name first appears in the Life of ST. COLUMBA as Arturius, son of AEDAN MAC GABRAIN, ruler of the Irish colony of DALRIADA in Southwest Scotland, who was slain in battle against the Miathi at Tigernach in 596.

Other mentions of the name testify further to the hero's existence. A late sixth-century Welsh poem by ANEIRIN, *Gododdin*, declares of a warrior at the Battle of CATTERICK that he "glutted the black ravens though he was not ARTHUR," and the late eighth-century *Expulsion of the Déssi* lists in a genealogy of those warriors who went to DEMED an "Arthur, son of Retheoir." The "Arthur son of Petr" in DYFED mentioned in the early seventh century may be the hero or he may, like the early seventh-century "son of Bicoir" or a late seventh-century ecclesiastic, simply be a namesake of the popular hero.

None of these instances of the name, however, establishes any connection between Arthur and his traditional connection with the Battle of MOUNT BADON. For that we must turn to the Welsh chronicler NENNIUS (c. 829), who in a *Historia Brittonum* identifies Arthur as the British hero of the battle against the Saxons (c. 500) at MOUNT BADON, a battle mentioned earlier by a British monk, GILDAS, in his *De Excidio Britanniae*, written only some fifty years after the event. He is called by NENNIUS a *dux bellorum* who fought alongside the kings of the Britons in twelve battles against the Saxons, of which MOUNT BADON was the last, on which occasion Arthur himself slew 960 of the enemy. In a later section of this same work, moreover, NENNIUS adds two revealing comments: that a stone bearing the footprints of Arthur's dog, CABAL, invariably returns to its cairn if moved and that the grave of his son, ANIR (cf. LOHOOT), always varies in measurement.

The Battle of MOUNT BADON is also listed as an entry for the "year 72" (c. 516) by the anonymous author of the tenth-century *Annales Cambriae*, where ARTHUR is said to have "carried the cross of our Lord Jesus Christ on his shoulders [possibly his shield] three nights and days," a detail appropriated from NENNIUS's account of another of Arthur's battles. The *Annales Cambriae* also mention the Battle of CAMLANN for the year 93 (c. 537) in which "Arthur and Medrawt fell," an indication perhaps that the skeleton of the full story existed in oral tradition at this time—500 years after Badon.

Other works—pseudo-histories like the chronicles of WILLIAM OF MALMESBURY, saints' lives such as that of St. Carantoc (cf. CARANNOG) and most notably Celtic TRIADS and works such as *Culhwch and Olwen* and *The Dream of Rhonabwy* (parts of the Welsh *Mabinogion*)—bear witness, however fragmentarily, to the development of the legend from NENNIUS to GEOFFREY OF MONMOUTH, as does such extraliterary evidence as the tradition, report-

ed by HERMANN OF LAON, that in 1113 nine canons of
Laon were shown in Cornwall the chair and oven of Arthur and that of the carving of the abduction of GUIN-
EVERE above the north doorway of the cathedral at
MODENA, both of which traditions bear witness to the international circulation of the Arthur story before its first
full treatment in writing—the *Historia Regum Britanniae*
of GEOFFREY OF MONMOUTH (c. 1136).

For in GEOFFREY's chronicle, whatever its sources, the
full story is first told: Arthur is conceived by UTHER
PENDRAGON upon IGERNE of CORNWALL with the aid of
MERLIN the magician, by whom he is spirited away until
he reappears to claim his throne. He subdues the recalcitrant petty kings of Britain and conquers nearly the
whole of Europe until, betrayed by his nephew MOR-
DRED, he is wounded in battle and taken away to AVALON
to be cured of his wounds.

In 1155, perhaps upon the commission of ELEANOR OF
AQUITAINE, the French poet WACE paraphrased GEOF-
FREY's Latin prose in French couplets and in doing so
added not only the ROUND TABLE and the hope of
Arthur's return, but also the courtly atmosphere which
later surrounds the legend.

Whatever his origins, the figure of Arthur is a figure
of romance as well as of pseudo-history. One sees in the
Welsh *Mabinogion* primitive hints of the world of the
chivalric quest fully developed in the romances of CHRÉ-
TIEN DE TROYES and his successors, where the ROUND
TABLE knights, particularly GAWAIN and LANCELOT, the
courtly lover of Queen GUINEVERE, assume the major
heroic roles, leaving Arthur the sole task of presiding
over the brotherhood.

Although the development of the Arthur legend can
be said to end with MALORY, whose great compilation
unites chronicle and romance traditions, the story is re-

cast in contemporaneous molds in nearly every age of English literature, in Tennyson's *Idylls of the King* an image of the collapse of the Victorian establishment, in Charles Williams of modern secularity, in T. H. White of the need of common standards of conduct and government.

Arthur, Son of Henry VII. Born September 19, 1486, and christened Arthur probably to connect Henry's Tudor ancestry with the Welsh Arthurian heroes.

Arthur and Gorlagon. Latin romance of uncertain date contained in a fourteenth-century manuscript together with *Historia Meriadoci* and *De Ortu Walwanii* which gives a cynical portrayal of women. Its account of Gorlagon's transformation into a werewolf suggests French and Breton sources.

Arthur of Daldriada. Son, or grandson, of AEDAN, ruler of Dalriada in the last quarter of the sixth century.

Arthur of Dyfed. Born of Irish ancestry, about the beginning of the seventh century, he is given different genealogies in the Irish ("Artuir maic Retheoir") and Welsh ("Arthur map Petr") accounts.

Arthuret. In Liddesdale, identified as ARFDERYDD, about eight miles north of CARLISLE.

Arthur's Bed. A group of rocky hills in CORNWALL.

Arthur's Chair. In CORNWALL, it was shown to a group of canons from Laon in 1113 according to HERMANN OF LAON.

Arthur's Cup and Saucers. Rock basins in the slate of a promontory along the coast of CORNWALL.

Arthur's Grave. In *Verses on the Graves* in the BLACK BOOK OF CARMARTHEN a grave for ARTHUR is said to be the most difficult thing to find or "the world's wonder."

Arthur's Oven. In CORNWALL, it was shown to a group of canons from Laon in 1113 according to HERMANN OF LAON.

Arthur's Wives. In the vast majority of accounts, GUINEVERE. According to the inscription over the tomb in GIRALDUS'

Speculum Ecclesiae, however, GUINEVERE was ARTHUR'S second wife, and in one possible interpretation of Welsh TRIAD 56 he has three wives, all named GUINEVERE.

Arthurus. Latinized name of ARTHUR in GEOFFREY.

Artorius. Name of a Roman *gens* occurring in Tacitus and Juvenal from which the name Arthur may have been derived. The "t" in the Roman name would have become "th" in Welsh.

Artuir. In the *Life of St. Columba* the son of AEDAN.

Artur. In the *Annals of Tigernach* for the year after ST. COLUMBA's death, listed as a son of AEDAN killed in the Battle of Circhind.

Astolat (Ascolat, Escalot), The Maid of. Carried in the Vulgate *Mort Artu* by a boat drifting to CAMELOT with a letter in her hand blaming LANCELOT for her death. Her name is usually given as ELAYNE LE BLANKE, and Malory identifies the place as GUILDFORD.

Âtre Périlleux. Anonymous poem in Norman dialect (c. 1250) relating characteristic adventures of GAWAIN. The name "Perilous Cemetery" comes from an episode in which GAWAIN, while spending the night in a cemetery, learns of a damsel imprisoned in a tomb.

Augwys. In LAYAMON and elsewhere, a king of Scotland, brother of LOTT and URIEN, who though at first hostile to ARTHUR later joins him and is killed in the war with MORDRED.

Aurelius Ambrosius. Cf. AMBROSIUS AURELIANUS.

Avalon (Avallonia, Avalun, Avaron). ARTHUR's final dwelling place, to which he is removed by three queens, having been wounded in the last battle with MORDRED from whence, according to legend, he will yet return to save the Britons. The name "Avalon" was thought by GEOFFREY OF MONMOUTH to come from *aval*, apple, and he describes this Island of Apples as a paradise where the fields need never be tilled and where grapes and apples abound. The Welsh texts also refer to the island as *ynys avallach*, Isle of Apples.

However, the name may be connected with one King ABALLACH who dwelt on an island with his daughters, one of whom was MORGAN. *Ynys avallach* may very well then be simply Avallach's Isle, and the connection with apples may have come through a confusion of *avallach* with the Irish *ablach*, "rich in apple trees," a term which was applied to the Hesperian island of Manannan the sea god. In time both notions seem to have been confused by the Bretons with the Burgundian Abbey of Avallon to create a beautiful island of apples with a legendary king and daughters (including, by a substitution, MORGAN for MODRON) fit to care for the wounded ARTHUR.

Later through a multiple confusion with the Hesperian Island of Apples and the Welsh Caer Wydyr (Fortress of Glass), Avalon became identified with YNIS GUTRIN (Glass Island), modern GLASTONBURY, an identification encouraged by the GLASTONBURY monks and by HENRY II and Richard I, both of whom wished to destroy the legend that ARTHUR would return to aid the Welsh and so supported the identification of Avalon with GLASTONBURY, where they in fact encouraged the monks to exhume and rebury what were thought to be the remains of ARTHUR and GUINEVERE. Other suggestions for the location of Avalon include Sicily, the Far East, Ninsavallan in CORNWALL, and various Welsh caves.

Avalon, Dame D'. In the *Prophécies de Merlin* along with other fays plots against LANCELOT, ECTOR, and LAMORAK. She also mocks the other fays after quarrelling with them and causing them to disrobe.

Avaron, Vaus D'. In *Joseph d'Arimathie* Petrus is to go to the vales of Avaron, perhaps the flat marshlands around GLASTONBURY, to await ALAIN's son.

Avowing of King Arthur, Sir Gawain, Sir Kay, and Baldwin of Britain. A poem (c. 1425) in tail-line rimed stanzas contained in a single manuscript composed probably in the north, and copied by a West-Midland scribe. It tells of the vows made by ARTHUR and these three knights after they had met a bear in Inglewood Forest and so is part of the extensive folk literature of boasting.

Awarnach. In Poem XXXI of the BLACK BOOK OF CARMARTHEN, a giant in whose hall ARTHUR kills a hag. Awarnach was later killed for his sword.

Awntyrs of Arthur at the Terne Wathelyne. A Middle-English late fourteenth-century alliterative romance. Written in Northwest Midland dialect, it is in two distinct sections, the first dealing with a ghostly appearance of GUINEVERE's mother to the queen and GAWAIN and the second, unrelated to the first, with the seating of GALERON.

B

Babylon. LUCIUS' kingdom in the GRAIL romances. It is not to be identified with the biblical Babylon.

Badon, Battle of. Cf. MOUNT BADON.

Bagdemagus. Cf. BAUDEMAGUS.

Baile in Scail (The Prophetic Frenzy [c. 1056]). Irish saga containing parallels to PERCEVAL's adventure at the GRAIL castle.

Bal(a)an. Brother of BAL(A)IN LE SAUVAGE, slain in combat by his brother in the *Suite du Merlin* and in MALORY.

Bal(a)in. In the *Suite du Merlin* deals KING PELLAM the "Dolorous Stroke" which lays waste the realm of LOGRES. In Tale II of MALORY's *Morte Darthur* called the "Knight with Two Swords" and in some accounts Balin le Sauvage, he is slain in combat by his brother BAL(A)AN.

Baldulf. A heathen, described in LAYAMON's *Brut* as "boldest of all knights" at BATH. WACE notes that he was skilled in harping "lais and melodies."

Baldwin, Bishop. Friend and counselor of ARTHUR. In the *Carl of Carlisle* along with GAWAIN and KAY he takes shelter in the hall of the CARL, a terrible giant, where he marries GAWAIN and the daughter of the CARL.

Baldwin of Britain (Bandewin). The principal figure in the *Avowing of King Arthur*. Arthur's Constable in Tale I of the *Morte Darthur*, he is made by MALORY in Tale II to assume MORDRED's usual role as regent during the Roman Wars.

Balor. One-eyed giant in Irish tradition. He is similar to YSBAD-DADEN in that his eyelids have to be opened by his servants.

Ban of Benoic (Benwick). In the *Lancelot* of the VULGATE CYCLE and in MALORY the father of LANCELOT and ECTOR. He helps ARTHUR defeat RION, king of the giants, and the recalcitrant vassals. BENOIC was probably in Western France.

Baram Downe. Barham Down near Canterbury, site of AR-THUR's second battle with MORDRED after MORDRED's men fled there from their defeat at Dover.

Barflete. In MALORY where ARTHUR lands on his way to fight LUCIUS. It is probably Barfleur in Normandy.

Bastard de Bouillon (c. 1350). French poem locating the resting place of ARTHUR and MORGAN in the East.

Bataille Loquifer (c. 1180). French work in which MORGAN and two sister fays transport a hero to AVALON, where he finds ARTHUR, GAWAIN, and YVAIN.

Bath. The site according to GEOFFREY of MONMOUTH of the Battle of MOUNT BADON.

Battle of Moira (Also the *Battle of Magh Rath* or *Cath Maige Rátha*). Second in cycle of three Irish medieval tales which tell the legend of SUIBNE GEILT, the wild man of the woods. In this twelfth-century account of seventh-century events, the sons of the King of Alba try to obtain from him the cauldron, "Caire Ainsicen," which never boiled over, yet always contained enough food for everyone according to his rank.

Baudemagus. Father of MELEAGANT in CHRÉTIEN'S *Lancelot.* A good king, his land of Gore is surrounded by water which could be crossed by only two bridges, one under the water, the other a sword with the sharp edge upward. The oldest of ARTHUR's knights, he is killed by GAWAIN.

Bawdewyn, Bishop. Cf. BALDWIN, BISHOP.

Bawdewyne. Cf. BALDWIN OF BRITAIN.

Bayen. Cf. BENOIC.

Beale Regard. In MALORY, the castle of MORGAN LE FAY.

Beauchamp, Richard de. Earl of Warwick whom Thomas MALORY may have served.

Beaumains. Name given in mockery to GARETH by KAY in MALORY's *Tale of Gareth.*

Beaume. Cf. BENOIC.

Beaurepaire. In CHRÉTIEN's *Perceval,* BLANCHEFLOR's castle.

Beauvais. In *Cligès* and *Perceval,* the cathedral library in which CHRÉTIEN claims he found his story.

Bede (c. 673–735). Saxon historian who wrote *Historia Ecclesiastica* repeats from GILDAS that the victory at MOUNT BADON (c. 493) stopped the Saxons' western expansion temporarily; he does not mention ARTHUR.

Bedegrayne, Castle of. Where ARTHUR's men were once beseiged. According to MALORY it is in Sherwood Forest.

Bedivere. First mentioned as Bedwyr in *Culhwch and Olwen* where he accompanies CULHWCH on his quest for his bride. Brother of LUCAN, ARTHUR's butler, and never a prominent knight in MALORY and later versions, he returns ARTHUR's sword to the LADY OF THE LAKE at the king's request. In LAYAMON he is killed in the battle near Langres when the Britons defeat LUCIUS and the Romans.

Beds. Both "adventurous," like that in the Vulgate *Lancelot*, where GAWAIN is wounded by a flaming lance, and "perilous," like that in CHRÉTIEN's *Lancelot*, where LANCELOT escapes a similar threat.

Bedwin the Bishop. In the *Dream of Rhonabwy* discovered by RHONABWY and Iddaug seated with ARTHUR on an island in the river.

Bedwyr. Cf. BEDIVERE.

***Bel Inconnu* (*The Fair Unknown* or *Guinglain*, c. 1190).** Written in the Île de France dialect, this poem partly by RENAUD DE BEAUJEU tells the story of GAWAIN's son, GUINGLAIN, who as a nameless young knight undertakes to deliver a captured maiden though he is reviled by her sister who accompanies him. The name of the poem is often used to designate a tradition of like stories, particularly MALORY's *Tale of Gareth*. Cf. LIBEAUS DESCONUS.

Belakane. In WOLFRAM's *Parzival* the black, pagan queen of Zazamanc in Africa. She is rescued by GAHMURET, and their marriage produces a son, FEIREFIZ, variegated in color.

Beli Mawr. Welsh king mentioned in early genealogies as ancestor-deity of Welsh dynasties, grandfather of BRAN and MODRON and brother-in-law of the Virgin Mary.

Bellangere le Beuse. Son of ALIXANDRE L'ORPHELIN. He avenges his father's death by killing KING MARK.

Bellinus. In GEOFFREY OF MONMOUTH early king of Britain.

Beloe, Lord of. In *Mort Artu* kills his wife because of jealousy of GAWAIN.

Benoic (Benwick). City and country of BAN. Usually placed in Brittany, MALORY identifies it as Bayen or Beaume in Burgundy.

Benoyce. Kingdom bestowed upon BOHORT by LANCELOT in the Vulgate *Lancelot*.

Bercheur, Pierre. Author of *Reductorium Morale*, which relates how the head of a dead man appears to Galvagnus (GAWAIN) on a platter in a mysterious palace.

Bercilak (Bernlak). In *Sir Gawain and the Green Knight* the Green Knight who plays the beheading game with GAWAIN.

Bernard of Astolat. In MALORY father of ELAYNE LE BLANKE, Lavayne, and Tinry, who offers LANCELOT lodging.

Bernlak. Cf. BERCILAK.

Béroul. Norman author of a fragmentary twelfth-century TRISTAN poem.

Bersules. KING MARK'S knight whom he sends to kill TRISTAN.

Bertholais. In the Vulgate *Merlin* chief conspirator of the plot to abduct GUINEVERE and substitute a false GUINEVERE as ARTHUR's bride. He is exiled along with the false GUINEVERE when MERLIN foils the conspiracy. In the Vulgate *Lancelot* GAWAIN offers himself as GUINEVERE's champion against Bertholais.

Bertram. In CHRÉTIEN's *Cligès*, the knight who detects CLIGÈS and FENICE together in an orchard.

Bertran de Paris. In a poem of instructions to *jongleurs* (c. 1200) mentions ARTHUR, TRISTAN, YVAIN, and MERLIN.

Beste Glatissant. The "barking" or "questing" beast, which MERLIN in the *Suite du Merlin* says is pursued in one of the GRAIL adventures. In MALORY he is pursued by PELLINORE and after his death by PALOMIDES. He has a serpent's head, a leopard's body, and the bay of sixty hounds.

Bicoir. The Father of ARTHUR the Briton in an entry c. 620–625 in the *Annals of Tigernach*.

Biket, Robert. Anglo-Norman poet who wrote *Le Cor*, sometimes called *Lai du Cor* (c. 1180), a fabliau-lai in verses of six syllables.

Birdoswald. Village on Hadrian's wall, known in Welsh as Camboglanna, sometimes identified as the site of CAMLANN.

Birth of Mongan. Possible Irish analogue of the begetting of ARTHUR.

Bisclavret (The Werewolf). Breton title for *Garolf*, one of the lais of MARIE DE FRANCE.

Black Book of Carmarthen. Twelfth-century book of Welsh poetry, some of which purporting to be the work of sixth-century bards. In Poem XXXI several exploits of ARTHUR, KAY and their followers are described, and in Poem XXII ARTHUR is mentioned as a leader in the Battle of Llanborth where GEREINT was killed. The manuscript is housed in the National Library of Wales at Aberystwyth.

Blaise. A fictional learned clerk to whom MERLIN in the Vulgate *Merlin* dictates the story of JOSEPH OF ARIMATHEA and the GRAIL along with all of MERLIN's exploits. He is often said to be MERLIN's master from birth. Cf. BLEHERIS.

Blancheflor, Mistress of Perceval. In CHRÉTIEN's *Perceval* the niece of the hero's tutor, GORNEMANT, with whom he spends the night "mouth to mouth" and whose enemies he vanquishes.

Blancheflor, Mother of Tristan. The sister of KING MARK of CORNWALL. She marries RIVALEN, a young noble, and dies in childbirth.

Bledri ap Cadivor. Twelfth-century Welsh chieftain sometimes identified with BLEHERIS.

Bleheri. Father of MERIADEUC in the thirteenth-century Île de France French verse romance *Le Chevalier aux Deux Épées.*

Bleheris (Bledhericus). Twelfth-century Welsh *conteur*, also called Blihis or BLAISE, mentioned by GIRALDUS CAMBRENSIS, THOMAS, and others as a pre-eminent story teller.

Bliant. In the Vulgate *Lancelot* takes LANCELOT to his castle and cures him of his physical ailments. He is later saved by LANCELOT when pursued by two knights.

Blihis. Cf. BLEHERIS.

Bliocadran (The Bliocadran-Prologue). An 800-line addition to

CHRÉTIEN's *Perceval*, sometimes called a prologue since it precedes CHRÉTIEN's poem in the manuscripts. Deriving its name from that given to PERCEVAL's father, it deals with the *enfance* of the hero.

Boarte. Cf. LOHOOT.

Bodel, Jean. In whose *Le Chanson des Saisnes* (end of twelfth century) are listed the three "matters": *de France et de Bretagne et de Rome la grant.*

Bodwyn. KING MARK's brother, father of ALIXANDRE L'ORPHELIN. His death at MARK's hand was avenged by ALIXANDRE's son BELLANGERE LE BEUSE.

Bohort de Ganys, King of Gannes (Bors). In the Vulgate *Lancelot* son of BOHORT OF GAUL, brother of LIONEL, and cousin of LANCELOT. Though induced by magic to lose his virginity, he nevertheless achieves the GRAIL.

Bohort, King of Gaul. In the Vulgate *Merlin*, brother of BAN and father of BOHORT DE GANYS. He is an ally of ARTHUR in the early wars.

Book of Taliesin. Thirteenth-century Welsh manuscript containing a poem (XXX) of earlier date, *The Spoils of Annwfn*, describing a raid made by ARTHUR upon ANNWFN, the Celtic "Otherworld."

Borre le Cure Hardy. Cf. LOHOOT.

Bors. Cf. BOHORT.

Boyhood Deeds of Finn. Irish story thought to have provided a basis for the *enfances* of PERCEVAL.

Bran de Lis. Fights a duel with GAWAIN in the FIRST CONTINUATION of CHRÉTIEN's *Perceval*.

Bran, Son of Aedan. In *Annals of Tigernach* in an entry for 598 listed along with ARTUR as one of the sons of AEDAN killed in the Battle of Circhind.

Bran the Blessed. The grandson of BELI MAWR. His father, Llys, is a sea-deity, and he is perhaps the prototype of BRON THE FISHER KING or Rich Fisher. Himself a deity, his exploits are miraculous and his severed head a ward against Saxon invasion.

Brandeles. In MALORY, one of ARTHUR's knights imprisoned by TARQUYN. Freed by LANCELOT, he fought in vain to prevent GUINEVERE's abduction.

Brandelis. Cf. *Gest of Sir Gawain.*

Brandigan. The island castle of KING EVRAIN in CHRÉTIEN's *Erec* where the JOY OF THE COURT adventure takes place.

Brandins (Brandue) des Illes. In the Vulgate *Lancelot* LANCELOT's enemy, the Lord of the DOLOROUS GARD.

Brangaene (Brangien, Bringvain). ISEULT's confidante, she arranges the love potion, takes ISEULT's place in MARK's bed, and is almost murdered by her mistress.

Brangoire. Father of girl who seduces BOHORT in the Vulgate *Lancelot.*

Brangore. In Malory, king of Strangore (South Wales) married to the daughter of the Emperor of Constantinople. At first an enemy, he is later an ally of ARTHUR.

Brangorre. King of GORRE in the *Prose Tristan*, he has been connected with the Welsh BRAN.

Branor le Brun. In the French prose romance T⸺ compilation of Rusticiano da Pisa (c. 1298) he, though 120 years old, triumphs over the champions of ARTHUR's court.

Branwen. One of the FOUR BRANCHES of the *Mabinogion*. Branwen, to whom one of "The Three Harmful Blows of the Island of Britain" was given in TRIAD 53, is the daughter of Llŷr.

Brecheliant. Cf. BROCELIANDE.

Bredbeddle. In *The Green Knight* the Green Knight who challenges GAWAIN.

Breguoin, Mons. Possibly High Rochester in the Cheviots, listed in the "Vatican recension" (944) in place of NENNIUS' MOUNT AGNED as the site of the eleventh battle of ARTHUR.

Brehus Sans Pitie. In *Palamedes* the knight to whom the revelations concerning the hero's ancestry are related. In the English romances he is called Bruns sans Pity. An enemy of ARTHUR, he is killed by GARETH.

Brenius. In MALORY an early king of Britain.

Breri. In THOMAS's *Tristan* cited as authority for KAHERDIN's and not GOVERNAL's acting as messenger to ISEULT. He is sometimes identified with BLEHERIS.

Bretagne. In the Middle Ages the name for BRITTANY or Great Britain before and during the Anglo-Saxon conquest.

Breunor le Noir. Named by KAY "LA COTE MALE TAYLE" in MALORY. DINADAN's brother, he marries MALEDYSAUNTE.

Bricriu's Feast. Eighth-century Irish saga containing two versions of the Challenge or Beheading Game motif, the "Champion's Bargain" and the "Terror," later to be used in *Sir Gawain and the Green Knight*.

Brisane. In the Vulgate *Lancelot* attends ARTHUR's court at CAMELOT with PELLES' daughter and GALAHAD.

Brittany. Province of Northwest France comprising the modern departments of Finistère, Côtes-du-Nord, Ille-et-Vilaine, Morbihan and Loire-Atlantique. Known to the Romans as Armorica, it is supposed that a large number of British Celts sought refuge there from the Saxons in the fifth and sixth centuries and so became known as Britannica Minor. It becomes the chief locale of the French Arthurian Knights, largely because the *conteurs* of Brittany were the chief composers of the early romances. BODEL in fact classified all Arthurian romances as the MATTER OF BRITAIN.

Broceliande (Brecheliant). Forest in BRITTANY visited by WACE (*Roman de Rou*) in the hope of seeing fairies ("A fool I returned, a fool I went; a fool I went, a fool I returned"). A magic wood nevertheless, it is the scene of adventures in CHRÉTIEN, the VULGATE CYCLE, and a number of French romances.

Bron (Hebron). In ROBERT's *Joseph* the husband of JOSEPH's sister, Enygeus, and the grandfather of PERCEVAL in the *Didôt Perceval*. He serves a single fish on the GRAIL Table and hence is called the Rich Fisher. Along with his twelfth son, ALAIN, and one PETRUS, he carries the GRAIL "westward," perhaps to GLASTONBURY. He is presumably the equivalent of the Welsh BRAN THE BLESSED.

Brulant. In the Vulgate *Estoire del Saint Graal* the king who kills the GRAIL King and causes a blight to come upon LOGRES.

Brumant. In the Vulgate *Lancelot*, nephew of CLAUDAS who is destroyed when he attempts to sit in the PERILOUS SEAT.

Bruns Sans Pity. Cf. BREHUS SANS PITIÉ.

Brut. Cf. WACE and LAYAMON.

Brut (Munich). Mid-twelfth-century chronicle of Great Britain in French verse sometimes identified as a fragment of the early portion of Geiffrei GAIMAR's last chronicle of the Britons.

Brut of England. Popular anonymous fourteenth-century prose work.

Brut y Tywysogion (The Chronicles of the Princes). Welsh continuation of the *Historia* of GEOFFREY.

Brutus. A descendant of Aeneas to whom medieval chroniclers attributed the founding of Britain.

Bryan de les Illes. Lord of the castle of Pendragon. He is an enemy of ARTHUR who imprisoned LA COTE MALE TAYLE until he was overcome by LANCELOT.

Buelt. In NENNIUS's *Mirabilia* the region in South Wales where the stone bearing the print of ARTHUR's dog CABAL can be found.

C

Cabal, Cavall. ARTHUR's dog whose grave in the region called BUELT was one of two marvels associated with ARTHUR recorded in NENNIUS's *Mirabilia*. When Cabal hunted TWRCH TRWYTH (in *Culhwch and Olwen*), he left his track on a stone which ARTHUR put on top of a cairn at Carn

Cabal ("horse's hoof"). When men carry it away at night, the stone miraculously appears back on the cairn the next day.

Cacamwri. In *Culhwch and Olwen* ARTHUR's servant who helped pursue TWRCH TRWYTH and was driven off "squealing and squalling" by the Black Witch.

Cadbury Castle. Cf. SOUTH CADBURY CASTLE.

Cadfan, Catamanus. King of GWYNEDD who died about 615. He was the grandfather of CADWALLAWN, and there is a memorial to him in the wall of Llangadwaladr church in ANGLESEY.

Cadoc, Saint. In whose biography, *The Life of St. Cadoc* (late eleventh century) by Llefris of Llancarfan, ARTHUR appears twice. In neither episode is ARTHUR shown in a favorable light, once impassioned by St. Cadoc's mother and later demanding unreasonable compensation.

Cador. Duke of CORNWALL in the *Dream of Rhonabwy* and a prominent figure in the chronicles of GEOFFREY, WACE, and LAYAMON, where he is a nephew of ARTHUR and the father of CONSTANTINE. He is killed in the last battle.

Cadwaladr of Gwynedd. The last of the British kings treated by GEOFFREY OF MONMOUTH. GEOFFREY may have confused BEDE's Caedwalla with the Cadwaladr of Welsh legend, who, along with CYNAN, is said in the *Armes Prydein* to be coming to drive out the Saxons. It is also possible that in that Welsh poem Cadwaladr was confused with his father CADWALLAWN.

Cadwallawn. CADWALADR's father who defeated the Saxons in 633. His battles are listed in the RED BOOK.

Caer Fandwy. A city, the name of which is unintelligible, from which only seven returned in the *Spoils of Annwfn*. The other cities so described, all of which probably refer to the "Otherworld," are Caer Veddwit (The Fortress of Carousal), Caer Siddi (The Fairy Fortress), Caer Pedryvan (The Four-Cornered Fortress), Caer Rigor, Caer

Goludd (The Inward Fortress), Caer Wydyr (The Fortress of Glass), and Caer Ochren (untranslatable).

Caer Leu. According to the *Bliocadran-Prologue*, the castle on the sea at Wales called Caflé by CHRÉTIEN (modern Dinlle) to which PERCEVAL's mother retired after her husband's death.

Caer Loyw. Prison in Gloucester from which MABON and Eidoel are released in *Culhwch and Olwen*.

Caer Oeth and Anoeth. Appears in TRIAD 52, "Three Exalted Prisoners of the Island of Britain," and in *Culhwch and Olwen*. In the latter ARTHUR is connected with this "castle of wonders." In the *Verses on the Graves* there is mentioned the *teulu* (warband) of Oeth and Anoeth.

Caer Seint. Latin SEGONTIUM, Roman fort at Snowdon on the site of modern CAERNARVON.

Caer Vaddon. Scene of the game of *gwyddbwyll* and the killing of the ravens in the *Dream of Rhonabwy*; possibly modern BATH.

Caerleon. Modern CHESTER, not to be confused with CAERLEON-ON-USK. Almost certainly the scene of ARTHUR's ninth battle in *Urbe Legionis* (The City of the Legions), so called because CHESTER was built as a Roman fortress by 78 A.D. for the Ninth Legion. The confusion arises from the fact that in some manuscripts it is called "Cair Lion," a name used in early Welsh histories to refer both to Chester-upon-Dee and CAERLEON-ON-USK in Monmouthshire.

Caerleon-On-Usk. Site of the Roman *Castra Legionis* at Isca which was established as a fortress for the Second Legion by 78 A.D. GEOFFREY made it the scene of ARTHUR's Welsh court (probably because of the ruins there), and it soon became the starting point of innumerable adventures.

Caernarvon. Near Snowdon in Wales, the site of the Roman fortress of SEGONTIUM.

Caesarius of Heisterbach. Recounts in the *Dialogus Miraculorum*

(c. 1240) that ARTHUR had been seen alive in Sicily in 1194.

Cafall. Cf. CABAL.

Cai. Cf. KAY.

Cai Cainbrethach. Legendary Irish figure in the TRIADS and saints' lives. He appears with BEDWYR as ARTHUR'S companion.

Caladbolg. FERGUS'S sword in *The Cattle Raid of Cooley*.

Caledfwlch. ARTHUR'S sword in *Culhwch and Olwen*.

Caledonian Forest. Cf. CELIDON.

Calibor(e). ARTHUR'S sword in the old French romances.

Caliburnus. ARTHUR'S sword in GEOFFREY OF MONMOUTH'S *Historia* and LAYAMON'S *Brut*. It is called EXCALIBUR in the romances and CALEDFWLCH in *Culhwch and Olwen* which appears to be the same as CALEDBOLG, the sword of FERGUS. According to GEOFFREY it was forged in AVALON.

Calles. In the Vulgate *Lancelot* defeated by his sons with the help of LIONEL and LANCELOT. His daughter healed LANCELOT and aroused GUINEVERE'S jealousy.

Calogrenant. In CHRÉTIEN'S *Yvain*, recounts to ARTHUR'S court his encounter with the Knight of the Fountain.

Camel River. Sometimes identified with the river Cambula on which ARTHUR'S last battle was fought.

Camelford. In CORNWALL, sometimes identified with CAMLANN, ARTHUR'S last battle.

Camelon. In Scotland, sometimes identified with CAMLANN.

Camelot. First mentioned in CHRÉTIEN'S *Lancelot*, the principal seat of ARTHUR'S court in the French romances. It was first identified with SOUTH CADBURY CASTLE by John Ireland in the sixteenth century, evidently on the basis of the village Camel, but the usual philological explanation is that it is CAMULODUNUM, now Colchester.

Camlann. The battle at which Arthur fought "with Medrawt," following the peace secured at MOUNT BADON. Listed in the *Annals of Wales* under the "year 93" (generally accepted as 537). In the Gwentian Code, the bard is told to sing the song of Camlann in a subdued voice in order not to excite the listeners. The traditional site of the battle is the CAMEL RIVER at CAMELFORD although it has also been identified as the Cam near Cadbury. In TRIAD 84, "Three Futile Battles of the Island of Britain," Camlann was the third and worst because it was brought about by such a "barren cause" as the quarrel between GWENHYWFAR and GWENHWY(F)ACH. Camlann is mentioned in the *Verses on the Graves* as the site of the grave of Osfran's son and with the Roman fort of BIRDOSWALD (Camboglanna in the kingdom of RHEGED) towards the western part of Hadrian's Wall.

Camulodunum. Roman name in Pliny's *Natural History* for Colchester which may have suggested the name CAMELOT to CHRÉTIEN, who first uses it for ARTHUR's court in *Lancelot*.

Capulu, Chapalu. Cf. CATH PALUG.

Caradawc. Son of BRAN in *Branwen, Daughter of Llŷr*.

Caradawg Vreichvras. Welsh form of CARADOC BRIEBRAS.

Carado. In the Vulgate *Lancelot*, carries off GAWAIN to the DOLOROUS TOWER. Eventually he is slain with his own sword by LANCELOT, who presents the head of Carado to ARTHUR.

Caradoc Briebras. Hero of the *Livre de Caradoc*, the FIRST CONTINUATION of CHRÉTIEN's *Perceval*. A serpent entwined itself around his arm as a punishment from his true father, an enchanter, when Caradoc informed his mother's husband of her infidelity. He was known as Caradoc "Short-Arm" or "Broken-Arm" after his arm was freed from the serpent.

Caradoc, King of Wales. In *Historia Meriadoci*, father of MERIADOC and Orwen. Caradoc is murdered by his brother, Griffith, who succeeds him. ARTHUR and URIEN defeat Griffith at Mount Snowdon and give the throne to MERIADOC.

Caradoc of Llancarfan. Contemporary of GEOFFREY and author of the alleged source of the Welsh *Brut y Tywysogion* and a Latin *Life of St. Gildas* (c. 1125), in which he records the story of ARTHUR's rescuing GUINEVERE (Guenmuvar) from MELVAS, who had carried her off to his home at GLASTONBURY. In the colophon to the *Historia* GEOFFREY asks Caradoc to write the history of the Welsh after CADWALADR.

Carannog, Saint. In *Vita Carantoci* (the *Life of St. Carannog*, early twelfth century), the missionary from Cardigan to whom God gave an altar which he set afloat on the Severn to indicate where he should go. He met ARTHUR who was searching for a serpent which was laying waste parts of Carrum, and in return for ARTHUR's locating the stone Carannog rid the district of the serpent.

Cardigan, Caradigan, Ceredigiawn. Norman name for the Welsh town ABERTEIVI, site of ARTHUR's court in CHRÉTIEN's *Erec*.

Carduel (Carlisle, Kardoil). Site of ARTHUR's court in the *lais* of MARIE DE FRANCE. It appears in CHRÉTIEN's *Erec*, *Yvain* and *Conte del Graal* and is the Welsh equivalent of CARLISLE, modern capital of Cumberland nine miles from the Scottish border on the Eden, Caldew and Petteril rivers. *Luguvallium* or *Lugubalia* in Latin.

Carduino. A late fourteenth-century Italian romance by Antonio Pucci which uses BEL INCONNU themes along with several motifs, particularly the widowed mother, seemingly taken from a PERCEVAL romance.

Carl of Carlisle. English rimed romance of about 1400 featuring an enchanted giant whom GAWAIN frees from enchantment by obeying his commands. The Carl gives his daughter to GAWAIN to marry and the Carl becomes a Knight of the ROUND TABLE. The poem features two motifs: the Giant's Daughter (a form of temptation story) and the Beheading Game.

Carlisle. Cf. CARDUEL.

Carmarthen. Site of the Roman fortress Maridunum.

Carmelide. Scottish kingdom of LEODEGAN, GUINEVERE's father in the Vulgate *Merlin*. In the Vulgate *Lancelot* ARTHUR is carried there by the men of the false GUINEVERE.

Carn Cabel. Cf. CABAL.

Carnwennan. ARTHUR's dagger in *Culhwch and Olwen*.

Carrado. An armed knight attacking Galvagin (GAWAIN) in the sculpture "porta della pescheria" on the archivolt over the northeast portal of MODENA Cathedral.

Cartelois. Castle to which GALAHAD, BOHORT, PERCEVAL and PERCEVAL's sister sail in the Vulgate *Queste del Saint Graal*.

Castel de Trespas. In the Vulgate *Lancelot* where YVAIN was imprisoned in the dungeon.

Castel Orgellous. (1) Where in CHRÉTIEN's *Perceval* there are said to be 566 ladies, each with a knight ready to joust for the prize, the best estate in the world. (2) A castle from which GIRFLET must be rescued by ARTHUR's knights in PSEUDO-WAUCHIER. The incident becomes one of the sources of *Golagros and Gawain*, a fourteenth-century alliterative romance.

Castle Dore. In Cornwall thirty miles south of TINTAGEL, the site of a pre-Roman fort of the first century A.D., later occupied in the sixth century. It has been identified as the palace of KING MARK because of its strategic location and because of the TRISTAN STONE.

Castle Mortal, King of. In *Perlesvaus* attacks the FISHER KING and takes the GRAIL Castle. He later kills himself when PERCEVAL retakes the GRAIL Castle.

Castle of Four Stones. In the Vulgate *Lancelot* where MELEAGANT's body lies.

Castle of Ladies. In CHRÉTIEN's *Perceval*, where GAWAIN passes the test of the PERILOUS BED. Later GAWAIN is told that the ladies in the castle are his grandmother, his mother and his sister. In the FIRST CONTINUATION of *Perceval* MORCADES is the queen of the Castle of Ladies and is GAWAIN's mother.

Castle of Maidens. In the prose *Tristan* the scene of the tournament at which DINADAN ridicules TRISTAN. In *Doon* the heroine is said to be mistress of this castle; in *Bel Inconnu* GUINGLAIN is lured to a tourney here; and in the Vulgate *Lancelot* GALAHAD delivers the captive girls to the Castle of Maidens. Since 1142 the site has been identified as the Castle at Edinburgh.

Castle of the Chessboard. For whose mistress PERCEVAL in the *Didot Perceval* procures the head of the White Stag.

Cath Palug, also Chapalu (Palug's Cat). A cat-like monster against which Cai polished his sword in Poem XXXI in the BLACK BOOK. This monstrous creature appears in the TRIADS and may be reflected in ARTHUR's killing a ferocious cat in the historical sequel to the Vulgate *Merlin*.

Catraeth. Cf. CATTERICK.

Catterick (Catraeth). In *Gododdin* the battle in which the Britons were defeated by the English.

Cauldron. Ancient Celtic vessel of magic and plenty. One with magic properties is found by ARTHUR in the "Otherworld" according to the Welsh *Spoils of Annwfn*, and in *Branwen, Daughter of Llŷr*, BRAN possesses a magic cauldron which, like Medea's cauldron, returns the dead to life.

In *Culhwch and Olwen* ARTHUR and his men seize the cauldron of DIWRNACH the Irishman and carry it off full of the treasures of Ireland.

In the Irish legend of the Tuatha de Danaan (Peoples of the Goddess Danu), the Dagda, the good god, has a Cauldron of Plenty (*Caire Ainsicen*), and in *The Battle of Magh Rath* the King of Alba has a similar cauldron. There are also Cauldrons of Plenty in the *Toghail Bruighne da Derga* and the *Tale of Mac Datho's Pig*. Some scholars believe the cauldron to be the origin of the GRAIL.

Cave Legends. Locate a sleeping, waiting ARTHUR at Mt. Aetna, Craig-y-Dinas, Llandegei, and Anglesey among other places.

Caw of Pritdin (Cadw of Prydein). A Northern ruler, father of
ST. GILDAS in the *Life of St. Gildas* in which one of Caw's
sons refused to obey ARTHUR and even harassed him
until ARTHUR killed him. Caw then prayed not only for
his son's spirit but also for his persecutor ARTHUR. In
Culhwch and Olwen Cadw of Prydein split in two the
head of Ysgithyrwyn, Chief Boar, and took his tusk.

One of ARTHUR's companions, in the *Life of St. Cadoc*
he is a giant.

Caxton, William (1422?–91). The first English printer, who
established his shop in Westminster in 1476, and who
printed in 1485 MALORY's *Morte Darthur* in response to
the demand of "many dyvers gentylemen of thys royame
of England." A number of modern students have alleged
that Caxton made editorial changes designed to change
MALORY's several romances into a single unified work.

Cei. Cf. KAY.

Celidoine. One of the sons of NASCIEN (Christian name for
Seraphe), the brother-in-law of KING MORDRAIN (EVALAC)
converted by Joseph in the Vulgate *Estoire del Saint
Graal*. Celidoine, succeeding NASCIEN, protected his people from famine and the Saxons.

Celidon, Celyddon, Cat Coit Celidon. A wood (*coed*) in Strathclyde possibly the *silva Celidonis* identified by NENNIUS as
one of ARTHUR's twelve battles. In other works, MYRDDIN
is said to have wandered there fifty years, hiding in an
invisible apple tree accompanied by a pig. Cf. *Hoianau*.

Celli Wig. ARTHUR's court and capital in the TRIADS and in
Culhwch and Olwen, possibly in CORNWALL, to which he
goes after driving TWRCH TRWYTH into the sea in the
latter work.

In the TRIADS (54) one of the "Three Unrestrained
Ravagings of the Island of Britain" occurred when
MEDRAWT went to Celli Wig, and in Poem XXXI in the
BLACK BOOK "savagery was experienced" when Celli was
lost.

In Cornish *celli* means a wood, and Celli Wig has been identified with Callington and Killibury among other places.

Celtchar, Luin of. The original spear of LUG which dripped blood when held aloft.

Cercamon. A twelfth-century Provençal troubadour poet who contrasted his faithless mistress with the faithful TRISTAN.

Cervantes. In *Don Quixote* (Pt. I, Ch. 13) first mentions the legend that ARTHUR was turned into a bird, a raven.

Champagne. A French district and former province comprising the departments of Marne, Haute-Marne, Aube, and Ardenne and parts of Seine-et-Marne, Meuse, Aisne, and Yonne. Its place in this dictionary is due to the fact that MARIE, the daughter of Louis VII and ELEANOR OF AQUITAINE, by marriage to Henri in 1164 became its countess.

Chapalu. Cf. CATH PALUG.

Chastel Orguelleus. Cf. CASTEL ORGELLOUS.

Château des Pucelles. In the prose *Tristan* where LANCELOT and TRISTAN are on opposite sides in a tournament.

Che. Name of KAY in the MODENA SCULPTURES, equivalent to French Ke.

Chelinde. TRISTAN's grandmother in the prose *Tristan*.

Chester. The site (*Urbs Legionis*) of the ninth battle of ARTHUR listed by NENNIUS. Cf. CAERLEON.

Chestre, Thomas. Author of *Sir Launfal* (c. 1350) and perhaps *Libeaus Desconus* (before 1340) and *Octavian*.

Chevalier à l'Épée. Written before 1210 in the dialect of the Île de France, this short romance recounts how GAWAIN is offered the daughter of his host, marries the girl, and later rejects her when she proves unfaithful.

Chevalier Aux Deux Épées (also called **Meriadeuc**). An early thirteenth-century romance composed in the dialect of the Île de France. Its hero, MERIADEUC, is occupied with avenging his father's death, while an extended subplot

deals with GAWAIN's attempt to find the missing MERI-
ADEUC.

Chevalier du Papegau. An anonymous fourteenth-century romance in prose dealing with a number of adventures of
ARTHUR himself, nicknamed the Knight of the Parrot.

Chèvrefeuil. A short lai (118 lines) of MARIE DE FRANCE composed about 1160 recounting an incident in the TRISTAN
legend. The love of TRISTAN and ISEULT is symbolized
by the honeysuckle twined about the hazel.

Chrétien de Troyes (fl. c. 1160–82). The first known writer of
romance, probably a native of Champagne. Nothing is
known of his life except that *Lancelot* (the *Chevalier de la
Charrette*), c. 1178, the first "courtly love" romance in
Northern France, was composed for MARIE DE CHAM-
PAGNE and *Perceval* (the *Conte del Graal*), c. 1182, the first
of the GRAIL romances, for Philip of Flanders. His other
romances are *Erec et Enide*, c. 1170, *Cligès*, c. 1176, and
Yvain (the *Chevalier au Lion*), c. 1178. Two songs and a
romance entitled *Guillaume d'Angleterre* are sometimes
attributed to him. While he almost certainly inherited
most of his characters and incidents from the oral Celtic
Arthurian tradition, his themes, particularly the relationship between love and marriage, and their effect
upon conduct of the courtly way of life, are distinctly his
own.

Citeaux. Site of Cistercian Abbey, the practices of which are reflected in the Vulgate *Queste*.

Clamadeus. In CHRÉTIEN's *Perceval*, the King whom PERCEVAL
defeats on behalf of BLANCHEFLOR.

Clarion. In the Vulgate *Merlin* King of the Saxons whom GA-
WAIN slays and whose horse, GRINGALET, GAWAIN takes.

Claris et Laris. A French thirteenth-century verse romance of
enormous length (30,370 ll.) describing the loves and
adventures of two knightly friends.

Clarissant. The sister of GAWAIN in CHRÉTIEN's *Perceval*.

Claudas. King of Terre Deserte, in the Vulgate *Lancelot*, who vanquishes BAN of BENOIC, LANCELOT's father. He is eventually defeated by BAN and BOHORT with the help of ARTHUR. In the Vulgate *Merlin* ARTHUR, GAWAIN, and MERLIN go to BAN's aid against CLAUDAS.

Cligès. The second of the romances of CHRÉTIEN DE TROYES, written about 1176. The first third of the poem recounts the love of the hero's parents, Alexandre of Constantinople and Soredamors, the sister of GAWAIN. The body of the poem deals with the love of Cligès and FÉNICE, the wife of his usurper uncle, Alis. He eventually steals her away after she feigns death and marries her upon the death of Alis. The poem is often said to be an *anti-* or perhaps a *neo-*Tristan.

Columba, Saint. Famous sixth-century Irish missionary about whom ADOMNAN wrote *Vita Columbae* in which there is mention of an ARTUIR, son of AEDAN. St. Columba was the founder of the monastery at Iona in the Hebrides.

Condwiramurs. In WOLFRAM's *Parzival* the wife of PARZIVAL and the mother of LOHENGRIN.

Constans (Constant). King of Britain in GEOFFREY OF MONMOUTH and in the Vulgate *Merlin*. The son of the first King CONSTANTINE, he is the brother of AMBROSIUS AURELIANUS and UTHER.

Constantine. ARTHUR's successor. The son of CADOR, he is designated by ARTHUR to succeed him in LAYAMON.

Conte del Brait (Li Contes del Brait Merlin). Missing work which took its name from the cry of MERLIN when he discovered he had been imprisoned forever in his tomb. *El Baladro del Sabio Merlin* is a Spanish version of this prose work which evidently was based on ROBERT's *Merlin* and parts of the PSEUDO-ROBERT *Merlin* continuation. In the PSEUDO-ROBERT cycle HELIE is mentioned as its author.

Conte del Graal. Cf. PERCEVAL.

Conte de la Charrette. Cf. LANCELOT.

Copper Castle. In the *Perlesvaus*, an enchanted castle which is guarded by two men of copper and which PERCEVAL takes.

Corbenic. The castle of the GRAIL, the original form of which was probably "Carbenoit," the castle of the "blessed horn," which demonstrates perhaps a confusion of *cors* "horn" with *cors* "body," a horn of plenty with the Blessed Sacrament.

Cornwall. County in Southwest England where Celtic civilization survived the invasions of the Saxons and where the events of ARTHUR's life are generally located, even in the Welsh stories. In GEOFFREY's *Prophetiae*, ARTHUR is called *aper Cornubiae*, "boar of Cornwall."

Cotovatre. In CHRÉTIEN's *Perceval* the lake near which lives the smith, Trabuchet, who made the sword given to PERCEVAL at the GRAIL Castle.

Count Ernols. In the Vulgate *Queste del Saint Graal* father of the wicked sons slain by GALAHAD, BOHORT, and PERCEVAL.

Crestiiens Li Gois. Author of the *Philomena* in *Ovide Moralisé*; sometimes identified with CHRÉTIEN DE TROYES.

Crône, Diu. Written c. 1220 by HEINRICH VON DEM TÜRLÎN. This long romance of 30,041 lines which deals principally with two visits by GAWAIN to the GRAIL Castle derives its title from the author's comparison of the events of the poem to jewels in a crown.

Crudel. In the Vulgate *Estoire del Saint Graal*, King of NORGALES who causes JOSEPH and JOSEPHE among others to be imprisoned when they try to convert him.

Cuchulain. The heroic young warrior of the Ulstermen in the Irish hero-tales such as the *Cattle Raid of Cooley* and *Bricriu's Feast*. His name means "the Hound of Culann." Like GWALCHMAI and GAWAIN he possesses qualities of a solar-hero.

Culhwch. Nephew of ARTHUR and hero of *Culhwch and Olwen*, in which ARTHUR is prominent as a huntsman.

Culhwch and Olwen. Contained in the *Mabinogion*, a Welsh

prose tale of the eleventh or twelfth century in which
ARTHUR appears as a British king, though quite unlike
the ARTHUR of the romances. A complete version of the
tale, which makes use of the folk motif of the Giant's
Daughter, is found in the RED BOOK OF HERGEST, an
incomplete one in the WHITE BOOK OF RHYDDERCH. The
story deals with CULHWCH's courtship of OLWEN, the
daughter of the giant YSBADDADEN, on whose land he
must with the assistance of ARTHUR perform a number
of tasks in order to furnish the nuptial feast and to
groom the giant for the wedding. The tale contains a
roll call of ARTHUR's companions.

Cundrie, Cundry. In WOLFRAM's *Parzival* GRAIL maiden who
curses and subsequently condemns PARZIVAL. She ex-
plicitly urges him to ask the redeeming question.

Cuneglasus. One of the five tyrants mentioned by GILDAS. He
is sometimes identified as an ally of ARTHUR.

Curoi Mac Dairi. Monster warrior who in *Bricriu's Feast* abducted Blathnat. He is slain with his own sword by CUCHU-
LAIN after Blathnat had stolen it.

Cyfarwydd. The title of a Welsh storyteller.

**Cyfoesi Myrddin a Gwenddydd ei Chwaer (The Conversation of
Myrddin and his Sister Gwenddydd).** Welsh poem found
in the RED BOOK OF HERGEST and in part in two other
manuscripts in the form of MYRDDIN's prophecies in
answer to GWENDDYDD's question.

Cyledyr the Wild. In *Culhwch and Olwen* takes the shears from
TWRCH TRWYTH.

Cynan. In the *Afallenau* of the BLACK BOOK one of two sons of
prophecy who are to deliver the Welsh. In *Armes Prydein*
(*The Prophecy of Britain*) and, later in GEOFFREY's *Prophetiae Merlini*, it is predicted that Cynan and his brother,
CADWALADR, will drive out the Saxons.

Cyprus. Part of the setting for the *Livre d'Artus*. The first
"ROUND TABLE" in which Arthurian figures were
imitated took place here in 1223.

Dagonet. ARTHUR'S fool in MALORY. In the Vulgate *Lancelot* he is merely a foolish knight.

Dalriada. Kingdom in Southwest Scotland and Northeast Ireland (present day Argyll and Kintyre) founded at the beginning of the sixth century by the Irish leader Fergus Mac Erc. According to ADOMNAN's *Life of Saint Columba* (c. 700), AEDAN MAC GABRAIN, who ruled Dalriada from about 574, lost three sons in battle, one of whom was ARTUIR, who according to one theory was confused in tradition with the victor of MÒUNT BADON.

Dame du Lac. Cf. LADY OF THE LAKE.

Danavexeria. Apparently Devonshire, where the group of canons from LAON were shown ARTHUR'S CHAIR and ARTHUR'S OVEN in 1113.

Daneborc, Danebroc, Tenebroc. French names for Edinburgh. Sometimes identified as the site of the CASTLE OF MAIDENS.

Danemarche, Queen of. In *Livre d'Artus*, traps ARTHUR'S knights within a wall of air. Her castle is called *Li Chastiaus des Puceles.*

Daniel vom Blühenden Tal (*Daniel of the Flowering Valley*). Written c. 1215 by Der Stricker, a miscellany of adventures derived from classical legends and several German writers including HARTMANN.

Dante Alighieri. Fourteenth-century Italian poet who, while not an Arthurian writer, includes in *The Divine Comedy* a few Arthurian references: to TRISTAN (Inferno V), to LANCELOT (Inferno V), and to ARTHUR and MORDRED (Inferno XXXII). There are also references to LANCELOT in the *Convivio* and to ARTHUR in *De Vulgari Eloquentia.*

David, King of Judea. Ancestor of LANCELOT and GALAHAD. In the Vulgate *Lancelot*, his sword lies on the bed in the ship built by Solomon to be sent (2000 years later) to the last

39

of his line in the *Queste del Saint Graal*. PERCEVAL'S sister weaves some of her hair with gold to form a girdle to hang the sword at the side of GALAHAD.

In the Vulgate *Tristan* TRISTAN is said to be descended from David and JOSEPH OF ARIMATHEA (confused here with Mary's husband).

De Amore. Twelfth-century prose work sometimes called *The Art of Courtly Love* by ANDREAS CAPELLANUS.

De Antiquitate Glastoniensis Ecclesiae (Concerning the Antiquity of Glastonbury Church). Written in the first half of the twelfth century by William of Malmesbury. An interpolator adds to the document that JOSEPH OF ARIMATHEA was in charge of the first twelve Christian preachers in Britain who had been sent from Gaul by St. Philip. Several stories connecting GLASTONBURY with ARTHUR were also interpolated from time to time in *De Antiquitate*, including that of YDER son of Nutt's killing three giants near GLASTONBURY and part of the history of the GRAIL.

De Excidio et Conquestu Britanniae (Concerning the Overthrow and Conquest of Britain). Written c. 540 by the British monk, GILDAS, who records the battle of MOUNT BADON but does not mention ARTHUR.

De Ortu Walwanii. Thirteenth-century Latin prose romance concerning the parentage, birth, and youth of GAWAIN. Like the *Enfances Gauvain* it follows a lost French romance in which ARTHUR'S sister is named ANNA, the Pope Sulpicious, and ARTHUR'S queen Guendoloena.

De Principum Instructione (Concerning the Instruction of Princes) (c. 1193). By GIRALDUS CAMBRENSIS, includes an account of the exhuming and reburying of ARTHUR and GUINEVERE at GLASTONBURY in 1191.

Dechtere, Dechtire. Sister of Conchobar, King of Ulster, and mother of CUCHULAIN by LUG.

Deheubarth. Southern Welsh kingdom covering approximately modern South Wales. Destregales (Estregales in *Bel In-*

connu), EREC's father's kingdom, is the French equivalent; both names mean "the right (hand) part."

Deira. Anglian kingdom in the Southern part of Northumbria, extending from Hadrian's wall to the Humber River. It is the site of the Battle of CATRAETH described in *The Gododdin*.

Deirdre. Heroine of *The Exile of the Sons of Uisliu* and wife of Conchobar, whose love for Noisi in the *Book of Leinster* parallels that of ISEULT for TRISTAN.

Demed. Cf. DYFED.

Déssi. Tribe from County Meath who settled in the territory of DEMED (DYFED) about the end of the fourth century. Its story is told in *The Expulsion of the Déssi*.

Desiré. Breton *lai*, probably based on MARIE's *Lanval* in which there are similarities between the story of Calatir and CHRÉTIEN's story of LAUDINE in *Yvain*.

Destregales. In CHRÉTIEN's *Erec*, EREC's father's kingdom. Cf. DEHEUBARTH.

Devonshire (Dumnonia). County in Southwest England. GEREINT in the *Gereint* is said to be King of Devon, and in *Culhwch and Olwen*, ARTHUR summons the men of CORNWALL and Devon for the hunt of TWRCH TRWYTH.

Dialogue of Arthur and Gwenhwyfar. Title given to poem appearing in a sixteenth-century manuscript recounting the abduction of GUINEVERE. The male speaker may well be MELWAS.

Dialogue of Arthur and the Eagle. Welsh poem, possibly twelfth-century (although it is found only in late manuscripts), in which ARTHUR and an eagle, the spirit of his dead nephew (who addresses ARTHUR as "chief of the battalions of Cornwall") engage in a religious discussion.

Dialogue of Myrddin and Taliesin (Ynddidan Myrddin a Thaliesin). Welsh poem probably slightly earlier than GEOFFREY OF MONMOUTH in which there is the only hint in Welsh literature not dependent upon GEOFFREY that

MERLIN had prophetic powers. The early date, however, is not exact, and the lines that suggest MERLIN's ability to prophesy may be a later interpolation, though it may have well been traditional.

Dialogue with Glewlwyd Gafaelfawr. Poem XXXI in the BLACK BOOK. Glwelwyd, ARTHUR's gatekeeper in *Culhwch and Olwen* and *Gereint*, asks who is at the gate. Arthur answers, "Arthur and the fair Cai" and then names his followers.

Diarmaid. Nephew of Irish chieftain FINN whose relation to GRAINNE, FINN's wife, and FINN is the same as that of TRISTAN to ISEULT and KING MARK. The legend, which existed in the ninth century, probably strongly influenced and shares many elements with the TRISTAN story.

Didot Perceval. Early thirteenth-century prose romance, named after an owner of the first manuscript, which continues the Vulgate *Joseph* and Vulgate *Merlin*. In it PERCEVAL emerges as the hero of the story of the PERILOUS SEAT and the GRAIL. One theory holds that it was based upon ROBERT DE BORON's verse *Perceval* with borrowings from CHRÉTIEN and the FIRST CONTINUATION.

Dillus Varvawc. In *Culhwch and Olwen*, whose death at the hand of CAI was probably the basis for the story of ARTHUR's slaying the giant RITHO in GEOFFREY's *Historia*.

Dinadan. Introduced in the prose *Tristan* as friend and companion of TRISTAN. A "laugher and japer" in MALORY, he mocks the chivalric code and rules of knighthood of the Arthurian world.

Dinas Emreis. In GWYNNED, below Castell Degannwg, the site of conflict between AMBROSIUS and VORTIGERN.

Dinas of Lidan. MARK's seneschal in Béroul's *Tristan*. The name stems from a misunderstanding of the Welsh *Dinas Lidan*, "large fortress."

Dindraither. Where ARTHUR rules in the *Life of St. Carannog*. It has been identified by some scholars as the Castle an Dinas near Crantock.

Dispute Between a Christian and a Jew. Late fourteenth-century poem telling of a vision of KING ARTHUR and his knights seen dwelling in a hall under a hill.

Diwrnach. In *Culhwch and Olwen*, owner of the CAULDRON which ARTHUR and his men sought in Ireland. He was killed by Llenllfawg with ARTHUR's sword CALEDFWLCH.

Dodinel. In *Claris et Laris* ridicules chivalry and knightly combat. In the Vulgate *Lancelot*, along with GUINEVERE and SAGREMOR he takes the wounded BOHORT to the Fairies' Fountain.

Dolorous Gard. A strong castle on the Humber, in the Vulgate *Lancelot*, whose evil enchantments can be overcome only by LANCELOT, who receives ARTHUR and GUINEVERE there and renames it JOYOUS GARD. However, after LANCELOT is forced to release GUINEVERE following her sojourn there after the death of GARETH, the castle again becomes DOLOROUS GARD.

Dolorous Stroke. Cf. BAL(A)IN.

Dolorous Tower. In the Vulgate *Lancelot* where CARADO imprisons GAWAIN. YVAIN and GALESHIN are also imprisoned there when they attempt to rescue GAWAIN. Eventually LANCELOT frees his friends and the Dolorous Tower is called La Bele Prise.

Domingart. One of AEDAN MAC GABRAIN's sons killed in battle in the *Life of St. Columba*. He appears also in the *Annals of Tigernach*, written a year after COLUMBA's death.

Draco Normannicus. Latin poem written in the second half of the twelfth century by Étienne de Rouen, a monk of Bec, whose subject is an expedition of HENRY II into BRITTANY. The material apparently comes only from GEOFFREY's *Historia* and *Vita Merlini*. Included is a letter from ARTHUR warning HENRY that he is in CORNWALL preparing to defend the Bretons, along with HENRY's reply that he will complete the conquest and then rule as ARTHUR's vassal.

Dream of Rhonabwy. In the RED BOOK, an early (twelfth century) prose tale uncontaminated by the French romances. Rhonabwy dreams of the eve of the battle of MOUNT BADON when all of the forces are gathering. ARTHUR and OWEIN, son of URIEN, play a game of *gwyddbwyll* involving squires and ravens. In the end a pre-battle truce is declared, and the author notes that the story cannot properly be told without his book, which correctly lists the colors of the chivalric trappings.

Dristan (Drystan). Name found in Welsh documents of about 1100. DRYSTAN MAB TALLWCH appears as one of ARTHUR's counsellors in the *Dream of Rhonabwy*.

Druas. Slain by AGRAVAIN in the Vulgate *Lancelot* in vengeance for a murder.

Drudwyn. In *Culhwch and Olwen*, "the whelp of Greid son of Eri," one of ARTHUR's men.

Drust. Son of Talorc, probably the Welsh DRYSTAN, son of Tallwch, in the TRIADS. This eighth-century king of the Picts was evidently connected with the legendary TRISTAN by the Welsh. Only in the Irish *Wooing of Emer* does Drust appear as a companion of CUCHULAIN; it is likely that he was the original hero of the story who rescued a foreign land from paying tribute and a princess from sacrifice.

Drustanus. For whom there may be a memorial stone, known as the TRISTAN STONE, a mile from CASTLE DORE in CORNWALL. The scarcely legible inscription reads, according to some scholars: "Drustanus Hic Iacit / Cunmori Filius" (Here lies Drustanus, son of Cunomorus).

Drystan Mab Tallwch. In the *Dream of Rhonabwy* one of ARTHUR's counsellors and lover of ISEULT. The name appears also in TRIAD 71 as "lover of ISEULT" and is probably the Welsh equivalent of DRUST, son of Talorc.

Dubglas (Blue-Black). River in *Regio Linnuis* where the second, third, fourth, and fifth of ARTHUR's battles listed in NENNIUS were fought.

Duke Ganor. In the Vulgate *Estoire del Saint Graal* converted by

JOSEPH in the beginning of the conversion of Great Britain.

Dumbarton (Alclud, Alcluith). Capital of Strathclyde, called "Castrum Arthur" in a 1368 document. It is mentioned in BEDE as a strongly defended town of the Britons.

Dumnonia. Cf. DEVONSHIRE.

Durmart le Gallois. First half of the thirteenth-century poem in which the hero wins a sparrow hawk contest on behalf of the Queen of Ireland (FENISE) whom he later marries. He rescues GUINEVERE but refuses to become a knight of the ROUND TABLE until he finds the Queen of Ireland.

Dyfed (Southwest Wales). Modern Pembrokeshire, settled about the end of the fourth century by the Irish DÉSSI from County Meath. One of the four states in the south that remained independent when Rhodri unified Wales in the ninth century, Dyfed, also called Demed, is the setting for the early episodes in *Culhwch and Olwen*. In GEOFFREY'S *Vita Merlini* MERLIN is King of Dyfed, and in the *Historia* MERLIN'S mother is the daughter of a king of Dyfed which, down to 1132, included CARMARTHEN.

E

Echoid Buide. In the *Life of St. Columba* the son of KING AEDAN and brother of ARTUIR who succeeded his father as king of DALRIADA.

Echoid Find. In the *Life of St. Columba* the son of KING AEDAN and brother of ARTUIR who along with ARTUIR was killed in the Battle of the Miathi.

Echtra. The ancient Irish term for "adventure" of which *Adventures of Art Son of Conn*, *Adventures of Cormac* and *Adventures of the Sons of Eochaid Mugedon* are examples.

Echymeint, Stone of. Under which ARTHUR, one of the "Three Exalted Prisoners of the Island of Britain" (TRIAD 52), was imprisoned.

Ector. In MALORY, father of KAY, foster father of ARTHUR.

Edern, Son of Nudd. Cf. YDER. Prince of Denmark, leader of the jet-black troops in the *Dream of Rhonabwy*.

Edinburgh (Teneborc). Cf. CASTLE OF MAIDENS. Probably Eidyn in the *Dialogue with Glewlwyd* and the *Gododdin*.

Edward I (1239–1307). In 1277 at Snowdon besieged and captured the fortress of the last native Prince of Wales, Llywelyn. This victory evidently served as a model for ARTHUR'S over Griffinus in *Historia Meriadoci*. In 1283 Edward was given the crown of ARTHUR, and in 1301 to support his claim to the kingdom he used among other arguments the one that ARTHUR had at one time held part of Scotland. At GLASTONBURY in 1278 he ordered ARTHUR'S tomb opened, and in 1299 his second marriage was celebrated with a ROUND TABLE at which his knights assumed the roles of ARTHUR'S knights in acting out episodes from Arthurian stories.

Edward II (1284–1327). First English crown prince to assume the title Prince of Wales.

Edward III (1312–1377). In 1344 formed an order of knights like that of the ROUND TABLE and in 1348 founded the Order of the Garter. This order of knighthood, however, had no Arthurian connection and had St. George, not ARTHUR, as its patron.

Eilhart von Oberg. An official of the Duke of Brunswick, Henry the Lion, who in the last quarter of the twelfth century wrote *Tristrant*, a German version of a lost French romance, evidently the same one used by BÉROUL.

Elayne. (1) In Malory, the Maid of ASTOLAT, commonly called LE BLANKE, who falls in love with LANCELOT; (2) in the Vulgate *Lancelot*, the wife of KING BAN, the mother of LANCELOT; (3) the daughter of KING PELLES, the mother of GALAHAD by LANCELOT; (4) the daughter of King Howel, killed by the Giant of St. Michel; (5) the sister of MORGAN LE FAY and MORGAUSE of Orkney; (6) in the *Didot Perceval*, GAWAIN's sister whom PERCEVAL loves; and (7) the wife of Persides in ROBERT's *Merlin*.

Eleanor of Aquitaine and Poitou (c. 1122–1204). Daughter of Willaim X of Aquitaine, married Louis VII of France in 1137 and in 1152 Henry of Anjou, who became HENRY II of England in 1154. Mother by Louis VII of MARIE DE CHAMPAGNE and Alix (1150), by Henry II of Guillaume (1153), Henry (1155), Matilda (1156), Richard (1157), Geoffrey (1158), Eleanor (1161), Joanna (1165), and John (1166). LAYAMON says that a copy of WACE's *Roman de Brut* was presented to Eleanor. Along with her daughter MARIE she was active in the cult of courtly love.

Eleanor of Castile (d. 1290). Spanish princess, first wife of ED-WARD I of England, for whom *Escanor* was written.

Eliduc. A *lai* (1184 lines) by MARIE DE FRANCE. It is perhaps the most famous example of the Man with Two Wives motif, which may have affected the development of the TRIS-TAN legend.

Élucidation. In the Mons manuscript, a prologue of uncertain date (484 lines) to CHRÉTIEN's *Perceval*. It is a confused piece relying heavily upon PSEUDO-WAUCHIER, incorporating a rimed table of contents of a GRAIL poem and an obviously Celtic folk tale of well-maidens. The author mentions the first two Continuations and cites BLIHIS as an authority that no one should tell the secret of the GRAIL.

Emer. CUCHULAIN's wife.

Emrys Wledig (King Emrys). AMBROSIUS in NENNIUS.

Enfances Gauvain. Early thirteenth-century French verse romance of which only two fragments (712 lines) survive, in which GAWAIN is the child of ARTHUR's sister MOR-CADES and her page LOT. After he is set adrift in a cask, he is rescued by a fisherman and brought to Rome, where he is educated and knighted by the Pope.

Englynion. Welsh epigrams, one of which is a dialogue in verse between TRISTAN and GAWAIN.

Engres. In *Cligès*, the count to whom ARTHUR leaves the regency of the kingdom while he goes to BRITTANY. Engres attempts to seize the kingdom and is besieged by ARTHUR at Windsor and defeated.

Enid. Daughter of Ynywl (Yawl, Nywl), wife of GEREINT in the Welsh *Gereint*. Having been won and wed by GEREINT, she later weeps the loss of his reputation through uxoriousness. Thinking her tears to be for another man, GEREINT rebukes her sharply and sets out on a series of adventures to regain his reputation in the course of which husband and wife are reconciled.

Enide. EREC'S wife in CHRÉTIEN'S *Erec*. Unlike HARTMANN and the author of *Gereint*, CHRÉTIEN provides no reason for EREC'S cruel treatment of Enide.

Enite. EREK'S wife in HARTMANN'S *Erek* in which she shares the blame for EREK'S neglect of duty toward the court and so deserves the harsh treatment she receives from EREK.

Enygeus. BRON'S wife, in ROBERT'S *Joseph*, whose son by him is to fill the empty seat at the table where JOSEPH assumes Christ's place at the Last Supper. One of their twelve sons is ALAIN who becomes the father of PERCEVAL.

Erec. Son of Lac, the hero of CHRÉTIEN'S *Erec*.

Erec. The earliest surviving Arthurian romance (5958 ll.) written by CHRÉTIEN c. 1170. It deals with the hero's winning of ENIDE, his loss of reputation through uxoriousness, and his consequent regaining of reputation through adventure.

Erek. By HARTMANN VON AUE, the first (c. 1190) Arthurian romance (10,135 lines) in German with the possible exception of EILHART VON OBERG'S *Tristrant*. It is based on CHRÉTIEN'S *Erec* and generally considered inferior to it.

Escalibor. Old French form of EXCALIBUR.

Escalon the Tenebrous. In the Vulgate *Merlin*, freed by LANCE-
LOT from a spell which enveloped his castle and church
in darkness.

Escalot, Maid of. Cf. ASTOLAT, MAID OF.

Escanor. French verse romance of 25,936 lines (c. 1280) written
by Gerard D'Amiens for ELEANOR OF CASTILE which por-
trays KAY in love and GAWAIN afraid to fight a duel with
Li Biauz Escanor de la Blanche Montaigne who accuses
him of murdering his cousin.

Escanor. In *L'Âtre Périlleux* carries off ARTHUR's maiden cup-
bearer. He is wounded by KAY, then slain by GAWAIN. He
carries a red shield, and his strength waxes and wanes
with the sun.

Escorant. The King of Sarras in the Vulgate prose *Queste* whom
Galahad is elected to succeed.

Étienne de Bourbon. In *Tractatus de diversis materiis praedicabili-
bus (Tract Concerning Various Praiseworthy Matters)* (1251–
60) told of a country man near Mons Cati who met some
men of ARTHUR's household who took him to a palace
where he saw knights and ladies.

Étienne de Rouen. A monk of Bec to whom is ascribed the
Draco Normannicus (c. 1168), a Latin poem which relates
the 1167 expedition of HENRY II into Brittany.

Evadeam. In the Vulgate *Merlin*, a dwarf who becomes a knight
of the ROUND TABLE.

Evalac. The King of Sarras in the Vulgate *Estoire* who upon
conversion adopts the name MORDRAIN.

Evrain. In CHRÉTIEN's *Erec*, uncle of MABONAGRAIN and king of
the island castle BRANDIGAN, scene of the JOY OF THE
COURT episode.

Excalibur. ARTHUR's fabulous sword (CALIBURNUS in GEOFFREY),
identified with the sword CALADBOLG wielded by FERGUS
in the Irish *Cattle Raid of Cooley*. In the Vulgate *Queste* it
is caught and brandished by a hand when it is thrown

into a lake after ARTHUR's battle with MODRED. In 1191 Richard I gave Tancred of Sicily a sword, Escalibur, which he said had been dug up at GLASTONBURY Abbey.

Expulsion of the Déssi. A history (second half of the eighth century) of the Déssi tribe from County Meath which settled in DYFED. Artuir maic Retheor appears in the genealogy of the rulers.

F

Feimurgan. In WOLFRAM's *Parzival* a country, apparently a mistake for Fée Morgan (MORGAN LE FAY) since the fay is named Terdelaschoye, Tere de la Joie.

Feirefiz. In WOLFRAM's *Parzival*, PARZIVAL's elder heathen halfbrother. He is variegated in color as a result of having a white father and a black mother, BELAKANE, a Moorish queen. He rides with CUNDRIE and PARZIVAL to the GRAIL Castle but as a heathen is not allowed to see the talismans. He becomes a Christian and marries a GRAIL damsel, Repanse de Schoye; together they go to India and become the parents of PRESTER JOHN.

Fenice. Daughter of the Emperor of Germany in CHRÉTIEN's *Cligès*. She feigns death in order to deceive her husband ALIS, CLIGÈS' brother, for the sake of CLIGÈS, whom she marries after the death of ALIS.

Fergus. French verse romance (6894 lines) by GUILLAUME LE CLERC (c. 1225). The hero is the son of a peasant who after being knighted falls in love with GALIENE, Lady of Lothian. He disappears after saving her from a siege and then appears again incognito at a tournament where GALIENE recognizes him. ARTHUR then gives him GALIENE in marriage.

Fergus Mac Erc. In c. 500 led a group from Ireland to found the kingdom of DALRIADA.

Fergus Mac Roich. Giant of Ulster warrior in the *Cattle-Raid of Cooley* who has a sword, CALADBOLG, which resembles ARTHUR'S EXCALIBUR.

Finn Mac Cumaill. Leader of an independent war band in the Finn Cycle, the Irish equivalent of KING MARK in the story of the elopement of DIARMAID and GRAINNE.

First Continuation. See PERCEVAL, FIRST CONTINUATION.

Fisher King. Term applied to the GRAIL keepers, among them PELLINORE, PELLES, and ALAIN, the "Rich Fisher." In CHRÉTIEN he is PERCEVAL'S cousin, in *Perlesvaus* and WOLFRAM's *Parzival* his uncle, in the *Didot Perceval* his grandfather.

Flamenca. Provençal romance (c. 1275) in which *jongleurs* recite CHRÉTIEN's poems at the wedding of Flamenca.

Flegetanis. Half-Jew, author of the history of the GRAIL which KYOT of Provence used and WOLFRAM cited in *Parzival*. A great astronomer, he said that he read the name of the GRAIL in the stars and that angels brought it down to earth.

Florée. Rescued from giants by GAWAIN in *Livre d'Artus*. She is the cousin of the heroine, Hermondine, in *Meliador*.

Florence. In MALORY, son of GAWAIN.

Floriant et Florete. French verse romance (8278 lines) of the second half of the thirteenth century in which the hero is carried off to MONGIBEL, Mt. Aetna, to be reared by MORGAN LE FAY. After rescuing his mother from the seneschal who had murdered her husband, the King of Sicily, Floriant marries Florete, the daughter of the Emperor of Constantinople. The story is unfinished.

Folie Tristan (The Madness of Tristan) **(Berne).** Early thirteenth-century Norman poem (572 lines) which like the *Folie Tristan* (Oxford) treats the section of EILHART in which TRISTAN in disguise as a madman visits the court of KING MARK to visit ISEULT.

Folie Tristan (**Oxford**). Late twelfth-century Anglo-Norman poem (898 lines) which deals with the same subject matter as the *Folie Tristan* (Berne) though at greater length.

Forest Perdue. In the Vulgate *Lancelot*, where an episode involving charmed carols and automatic chessmen occurs.

Fouke Fitz Warin. Verse romance written in Shropshire (c. 1255) relating an incident concerning Cahus, ARTHUR'S squire, found in Branch I of *Perlesvaus*.

Four Ancient Books of Wales. W. F. Skene's edition and translation of the early Welsh verse of THE BLACK BOOK OF CARMARTHEN, THE BOOK OF ANEIRIN, THE BOOK OF TALIESIN, and THE RED BOOK OF HERGEST.

Four Branches of the Mabinogion. Pwyll, Prince of Dyfed; Branwen, Daughter of Llŷr; Manawydan, Son of Llŷr; and Math, Son of Mathonwy. These four tales constitute the *Mabinogion* proper and deal with the exploits of Prince Pryderi.

Frederick II, Emperor (1194–1250). Called the "Stupor Mundi," Hohenstaufen Emperor of the Holy Roman Empire and King of the Kingdom of Two Sicilies. In a letter dated February 5, 1240 he thanked the Segreto of Messina for a copy of *Palamedes*. According to the prologue of the *Prophécies de Merlin*, Frederick commanded Maistre Richart d'Islande to translate the work from Latin into French.

Frederick Barbarossa (1122–90). German emperor, whose attempt to marry the daughter of the Greek Emperor Comnenus may have suggested the German-Greek marriages of *Cligès*. His victory at Connelant may have been reflected in HARTMANN'S substituting Conne-Iconium for the town in his source. A legend of survival grew up around him as around ARTHUR.

Frenzy of Suibne. Irish tale of life of SUIBNE GEILT in the woods after he went mad in the Battle of Moira (673).

Froille d'Alemaigne. In the Vulgate *Merlin* along with CLAUDAS de la Deserte and others invades BAN'S kingdom of

BENOIC. In the Vulgate *Lancelot* he challenges ARTHUR to a duel in which he is killed. In the Vulgate *La Mort Artu* the emperor of the Romans comes to arrange Froille's death and is killed by ARTHUR. Cf. FROLLO.

Froissart, Jean. Author of *Meliador*. From 1361–68 he served in the household of Edward III, and in 1369 Wencelas, Duke of Luxembourg, became his patron and commissioned him to write *Meliador*.

Frollo. In GEOFFREY's *Historia* a Roman tribune of Gaul whom ARTHUR killed in single combat. See FROILLE.

Füetrer, Ulrich. Author of *Buch der Abenteuer* (c. 1490), a collection of *Romane* which contains *inter alia* an adaptation of WOLFRAM's *Parzival*.

G

Gaheret. Possibly the third son of LOT, so often confused with his brothers GAHERIS and GARETH that it seems doubtful that he has a separate existence except in MALORY where he is said to fight against the heathen invaders.

Gaheris. Fourth son of LOT, the youngest in those works where GARETH does not appear. Although often confused with GAHERET, he is in the VULGATE CYCLE and in MALORY the murderer of MORGAUSE, his mother, whom he discovers in bed with LAMORAK, and he is later accidentally killed along with GARETH during LANCELOT's ill-fated rescue of GUINEVERE.

Gahmuret. Prince of ANJOU, PARZIVAL's father in WOLFRAM's *Parzival* and father by BELAKANE of FEIREFIZ. Through his marriage to HERZELOYDE, by whom he fathered PARZIVAL, he became King of Wales.

Gaimar, Geffrei. Author of *L'Estoire des Engles* (c. 1145), a verse adaptation of GEOFFREY's *Historia* to which he added the history to the time of William Rufus.

Galahad, Galaad. The immaculate GRAIL hero, son of LANCELOT and ELAYNE, the daughter of PELLES, the GRAIL King. In the VULGATE CYCLE and in MALORY a symbol of the potential union of secular perfection and holiness, he "achieves" the PERILOUS SEAT of the ROUND TABLE and later the GRAIL itself at the Castle of CORBENIC, performs a number of miracles, and departs with the vessel to the holy land of SARRAS.

Galatyn, Galantyne. In MALORY, GAWAIN's sword.

Galehaudin. In the VULGATE *Lancelot*, nephew of GALEHAUT who succeeds him.

Galehaut, Galeatt, Galahault. In the VULGATE *Lancelot*, prince of the Lointaines Isles who invades ARTHUR's kingdom after ARTHUR refuses to yield to him. He becomes LANCELOT's friend and arranges the secret meeting between LANCELOT and GUINEVERE which is the beginning of their love affair. GUINEVERE in turn arranges a tryst in which Galehaut and Lady of Malehaut become lovers. When Galehaut hears the false report of LANCELOT's death, he dies of grief, and the Lady of Malehaut in turn dies lamenting Galehaut. The section of the *Lancelot* concerning him forms a complete story which is known as the *Galehaut*.

Galeran de Bretagne. Assigns to the Bretons the tradition that ARTHUR was killed by a monstrous cat.

Galeron. GALVARIUM in the MODENA SCULPTURE, the second knight mounted from the right riding to help GALVAGINUS against CARRADO.

Galeron. In the *Awntyrs of Arthur* a Scottish knight claiming land whom GAWAIN fights. He renounces his claim when almost defeated and becomes a ROUND TABLE knight.

Gales. Old French for Wales, which perhaps influenced naming of GALAHAD and GALEHAUT.

Galfridus Artur. GEOFFREY's signature in the *Historia*.

Galiene. In *Fergus*, the Lady of Lothian who recognizes the disguised FERGUS at ARTHUR's tournament at Gedeorde. She requests FERGUS as her husband, and the poem ends with their marriage at Roxburgh.

Galinguefort (Wallingford). In CHRÉTIEN's *Cligès*, the site of one of ARTHUR's tourneys.

Galoche. In *Sone de Nausay*, an island castle of monks where Sone was shown the GRAIL and other holy relics. The name may be a corruption of Old French *Galesche* (Welsh).

Galvaginus. On the MODENA SCULPTURE the foremost knight, GAWAIN. In *Reductorium Morale*, Galvaginus sees the severed head of a dead man on a platter and a giant lying near the fire.

Galvarium. A knight, GALERON, on the MODENA SCULPTURE.

Gandin. In WOLFRAM's *Parzival*, GAHMURET's father.

Ganieda. In the *Vita Merlini*, MERLIN's sister who marries Rodarchus, King of Cumberland. After her husband's death she vows to join her brother in the wilderness. She becomes a prophet and the poem ends with her prophecies which refer to political events of the 1140's. In Welsh literature her name is GWENDDYDD.

Gannes. In the Vulgate *Lancelot*, BOHORT's kingdom, which CLAUDAS seizes; also the scene of a battle in the war with CLAUDAS. LANCELOT later gives Gannes to LIONEL.

Garel vom Blühenden Tal. Late thirteenth-century poem, a reworking of HARTMANN's *Daniel* by Der Pleier containing in its 12,304 verses little Arthurian material.

Gareth. Also called BEAUMAINS in MALORY, the youngest of LOT's sons, where in one of the best-known BEL INCONNU adventures he rescues and weds the Lady LYONES. Sponsored as a young knight by LANCELOT, he is accidentally struck down by LANCELOT in his ill-fated rescue of GUINEVERE following the treachery of AGRAVAIN and MORDRED. Gareth's death brings on the irrational anger of GAWAIN which results in the final tragedy.

Gaucher de Dourdan. Cf. WAUCHIER DE DENAIN.

Gautier de Montbéliard. Journeyed to Palestine in 1199 where he became Constable of Jerusalem and later Regent of Cyprus. In ROBERT's *Joseph d'Arimathie*, he appears as ROBERT's lord, "Gautier . . . de Mont Belyal" (Montbéliard).

Gauvain. Cf. GAWAIN.

Gawain. (*Fr.* Gauvain [Gaugain], *Lat.* Gualganus, Walganus, *W.* Gwalchmei "hawk or falcon of May," *Br.* Walchmoe). The principal hero of the Arthurian romances. Perhaps originally a Celtic sun god, he is in the story the nephew of ARTHUR, the eldest son of LOT (GWYAR in *Culhwch and Olwen*) and MORGAUSE of Orkney (ANNA in GEOFFREY) and brother, in the English tradition to AGRAVAIN, GAHERIS, GARETH, and the traitor MODRED. He dies when ARTHUR returns from the continent to fight the usurper. Though for the most part a fearless knight, he at times has a reputation for lechery and treachery as well as for courtesy, the Gawain "light in life and light in death" of Tennyson. A number of the romances, notably *Sir Gawain and the Green Knight* and MALORY's *Morte Darthur* thus present him as a mixed character.

Genewis. Kingdom of PANT, LANCELOT's father in *Lanzelet*. It is probably a variation of the Welsh name for North Wales, "Gwynedd." It may be, however, that it corresponds to Benok in the Vulgate *Lancelot* and that both are corruptions òf the French adjective for "blessed."

Geoffrey of Monmouth. (c. 1100–c. 1155). The most influential of the English Arthurian chroniclers, the first to record in skeletal form the whole life of ARTHUR. A Welsh cleric (later Bishop of St. Asaph), he wrote a *Prophetiae Merlini* or *Libellus Merlini* (c. 1135), the *Historia Regum Britanniae* (c. 1136, though the first of his works begun), and the *Vita Merlini* (c. 1151). All three rely upon oral Welsh sources as well as their author's imagination, but the

Historia, the most important of the three, names as a source a "very old book in the British language" given Geoffrey by one Walter, Archdeacon of Oxford. The evidence is all against the existence of such a book, and Geoffrey's chief sources would seem to be BEDE, GILDAS, and NENNIUS and, for the ARTHUR material, Welsh tradition. Though he traces the early history of the Britons, Geoffrey's concentration on the hitherto unrecorded ARTHUR indicates that his chief purpose was to celebrate him, perhaps in order to produce a native British hero to rival the French Charlemagne. Whatever his purpose, his success was enormous. Translated into French by WACE, into English by LAYAMON, and reflected in innumerable chronicles, its version of the Arthurian tragedy became the scaffold upon which later writers built.

Gerbert de Montreuil. Author of *Roman de la Violette*, to whom is attributed the redaction (17,000 lines) of a continuation of CHRÉTIEN's *Perceval* about 1230. The redaction appears in two manuscripts between the SECOND CONTINUATION and MANESSIER's conclusion. He has PERCEVAL achieve the GRAIL adventure, marry BLANCHEFLOR, and become the father of the Swan Knight and of the three conquerors of Jerusalem.

Geraint, Son of Erbin. Poem in the BLACK BOOK in which ARTHUR is "emperor and conductor" in the battle of LLONGBORTH in which the hero was killed.

Gereint. Sixth-century King of Dumnonia, son of Erbin, subject of a poem, one version of which appears in the BLACK BOOK, another in the RED BOOK. It appears that ARTHUR fought on his side in a battle at LLONGBORTH. The name was possibly derived from the Latin Gerontius (in *Culhwch and Olwen*, father of Cadwy and OLWEN).

Gereint. Thirteenth-century Welsh prose tale in the *Mabinogion* which corresponds to CHRÉTIEN's *Erec* and which probably derives from a common source. It differs from *Erec* only in detail and in ascribing Gereint's cruelty to ENID to jealousy.

Gerontius. The last independent Celtic King of Dumnonia, possibly GEREINT. He was defeated by Ina of Wessex in 710 A.D.

Gervase of Tilbury. About 1215 wrote *Otia Imperialia* in which he recorded the Sicilian legend that ARTHUR had been seen in the lower parts of Mt. Aetna. He adds that he had heard similar stories in Britain. This is the earliest record of the tradition that ARTHUR is alive and will return.

Gest of Sir Gawain. C. 1450 English rimed romance of which only a fragment (541 ll.) survives. The poet retells in an altered version the seduction of Brandelis' sister by GAWAIN and the duel between Brandelis and GAWAIN found in the FIRST CONTINUATION of CHRÉTIEN'S *Conte del Graal.*

Gesta Pilati (The Deeds of Pilate). The first part of *Evangelium Nicodemi* which ROBERT used to form his history of the GRAIL.

Geste des Bretons (The Deeds of the Bretons). WACE'S own title for his poem commonly known as *Brut.*

Giflet, Girflet, Griflet. Appears in *Lai du Cor* and in CHRÉTIEN'S *Perceval.* In the FIRST CONTINUATION of CHRÉTIEN'S *Perceval* he appears as Girflet, son of Do, and undertakes the adventure of the CASTEL ORGUELLOUS. In the Vulgate *Mort Artu* after accompanying the wounded ARTHUR to the sea, he disobeys ARTHUR'S first two commands to throw EXCALIBUR into the lake, then upon obeying, sees a hand rise from the water to grasp the sword. He discovers ARTHUR'S body a few days later in the Noire Chapelle.

Gildas (c. 516–570). Welsh monk born probably near Glasgow who in *De Excidio Britanniae* (c. 540) tells how the Britons defeated the Saxons at the siege of MOUNT BADON, the battle which NENNIUS later associates with ARTHUR. There is confusion surrounding the date of the battle since Gildas seems to place it as happening forty years before his writing, but his exact intentions are not clear. He is certainly more interested in praising the Romans to the detriment of his British contemporaries than in presenting an accurate account of history. A *Vita Gildae* written much later tells of the quarrel between ARTHUR (*rex rebellis*) and HUEIL, Gildas' brother, which resulted in ARTHUR's killing HUEIL.

A medieval tradition recognized two Gildases—Gildas Albanius, the Saint, and Gildas Badonicus, the historian.

Ginglain. Cf. GUINGLAIN.

Giraldus Cambrensis. (c. 1145–c. 1220). Welsh ecclesiastic, author of *Topographia Hibernica* (c. 1185), *Descriptio Cambriae* (c. 1198), *Itinerarium Cambriae* (c. 1168), *De Instructione Principum* (c. 1193), *Speculum Ecclesiae* (c. 1218), in which he distinguishes between MERLIN Ambrosius and MERLIN Sylvester and implies that GEOFFREY's book is false. In *De Instructione Principum*, he gives an account of the discovery of ARTHUR's grave at GLASTONBURY, including the leaden cross discovered under a stone beneath the coffin and inscribed "Hic jacet sepultus inclitus rex Arthurus cum Wenneveria uxore sua secunda in insula Avallonia," (Here lies buried the famous King ARTHUR with GUINEVERE his second wife on the island Avalon).

Girard D'Amiens. Late thirteenth-century author of *Escanor*.

Glais, Gais, Gals. PERCEVAL's paternal grandfather in *Perlesvaus*.

Glasteing. In *De Antiquitate Glastonensis Ecclesiae* of WILLIAM OF MALMESBURY one of the twelve brothers who came from the North of Britain into the West. According to WILLIAM or, rather, an interpolator, GLASTONBURY (Glastinbery) took its name from Glasteing.

Glastonbury. Abbey in Somerset deeply involved in a number of Arthurian matters: (1) once an island, it has been identified, principally through a philological confusion, with AVALON, and indeed the abbey monks at the suggestion of HENRY II excavated in 1191 a number of bones together with a lead cross identifying the remains of ARTHUR and GUINEVERE; (2) according to *Vita Gildae* of CARADOC OF LLANCARFAN (c. 1138) MELWAS, King of the Summer Country, abducted GUINEVERE to Glastonbury; (3) ROBERT DE BORON in the *Joseph* states that BRON, called the Rich Fisher, the brother-in-law of JOSEPH OF ARIMATHEA, carried the GRAIL to Glastonbury, the "vale of Avaron." A grave reputed to be the reburial place of ARTHUR and a miraculous thorn tree grown from JOSEPH's staff may still be seen. Excavation has given some support to the stories of Arthur's grave and the citadel of Melwas.

Glatysaunt Beest. Cf. BESTE GLATISSANT.

Glein, River. Site of ARTHUR's first battle in NENNIUS. This may be River Glen in Lincolnshire or in Northumberland.

Gliglois. Written in the first half of the thirteenth century, an anonymous poem of 2942 lines telling the story of Gliglois, the son of a German noble who comes to ARTHUR's court. He becomes squire to GAWAIN who has him enter into the service of Beauty, whom GAWAIN loves. Gliglois and Beauty fall in love and eventually marry. The supernatural is missing in this poem, which evidently gives a faithful representation of contemporary society.

Glwelwyd Gafaelfawr. Gatekeeper in Poem XXXI in the BLACK BOOK. In *Culhwch and Olwen* and in *Gereint* he is the porter at ARTHUR's court.

Godfrey of Bouillon. (c. 1060–c. 1100). Hero of the First Crusade, alluded to as a descendent of PERCEVAL and BLANCHEFLOR in GERBERT's continuation. The house of Bouillon was connected with the Swan Knight.

Godfrey of Lagny (Leigni). At the request of CHRÉTIEN wrote the last thousand lines of *Lancelot*. He mentions Bade (BATH) as the capital of GORRE.

Godfrey of Viterbo. Secretary to FREDERICK BARBAROSSA (c. 1200) who referred to the expectation of ARTHUR'S return.

Gododdin. Contained in *The Book of Aneirin*, a Welsh elegy dating in original form from the sixth century noting that at the battle of CATRAETH GWAWRDDUR "glutted the black ravens though he was not ARTHUR."

Gogrvan Gawr. GUINEVERE's father in Welsh literature.

Golagros and Gawain. Late fifteenth-century Scottish alliterative romance relating two episodes from the FIRST CONTINUATION of CHRÉTIEN's *Conte del Graal*. Here BRANDELIS is named Spinagros and the Riche Soudoier Golagros.

Golden Circlet. Christ's crown of thorns which PERCEVAL wins as a prize in the *Perlesvaus* when he frees the castle of the Golden Circlet from the Knight of the Burning Dragon.

Gomeret. A kingdom in CHRÉTIEN's *Erec*; a kingdom or personal name in other romances. It may be the model for the name of PERCEVAL's father, GAHMURET, in WOLFRAM's *Parzival*.

Gonnot, Michel. Scribe who compiled (c. 1470) a compendium of prose romances for the Duc de Nemours, JACQUES D'ARMAGNAC, including the VULGATE *Lancelot*.

Gonosor. The King of Ireland in the prose *Tristan*. The name may be a corruption of Nabugodonosor, the Vulgate Bible version of Nebuchadnezzar.

Good Fisher. In ROBERT's *Joseph*, JOSEPH's brother, BRON, the keeper of the GRAIL. He is also called the Rich Fisher as in CHRÉTIEN's *Perceval*.

Goon Desert. In MANESSIER's continuation of CHRÉTIEN's *Perceval*, brother of the Fisher King. In *Peredur* his head instead of the wafer appears on the dish.

Gorlois. Duke of CORNWALL, husband of IGERNE in GEOFFREY.

UTHER, assuming his likeness with the help of MERLIN's magic, goes to his castle at TINTAGEL and begets ARTHUR. After Gorlois is killed UTHER marries IGERNE.

Gornemant de Gohort. BLANCHEFLOR's uncle in CHRÉTIEN's *Conte del Graal*. He gives PERCEVAL training in knighthood and knights him, but his warning against loquacity prevents PERCEVAL's asking questions at the GRAIL castle. In GERBERT's continuation he is confused with the FISHER KING.

Gorre, Gore. In CHRÉTIEN's *Lancelot*, the Kingdom of BAUDEMAGUS surrounded by water, which can be reached by only two bridges—one a sword, the other underwater. In GODEFROI's continuation BATH (Bade) is mentioned as its capital, and in MALORY, it is said to be the kingdom of URIEN. It is sometimes identified as GLASTONBURY. Cf. BRANGORRE.

Gorvenal, Governayle. The knight who instructs TRISTAN in knighthood and goes with him to MARK's court where he serves as TRISTAN's messenger to ISEULT.

Gottfried von Strassburg. Wrote *Tristan*, (c. 1210) following THOMAS of Britain, but emphasizing, as his source did not, the passion of the lovers. The poet did not finish the episode of ISEULT OF THE WHITE HANDS. Together with WOLFRAM he represents the height of the German medieval courtly epic.

Graelent. Breton *lai*, a variant of the *Lanval* story, of MARIE DE FRANCE with Arthurian setting in which the queen, not named, is contemptible.

Grail, Holy. The most controversial and intriguing of Arthurian matters. Mythologically it is said to be the vessel from which Christ drank at the Last Supper and, occasionally, the cup used by the centurion Longinus to catch the blood of Christ on the cross. What is later to be identified as the Grail first appears in written literature as a *graal*, a shallow dish, carried by a maiden in a procession witnessed by PERCEVAL in CHRÉTIEN's *Perceval*. Here it is said to sustain miraculously the wounded FISHER KING whose sterility has laid waste his country. The first of CHRÉTIEN'S continuators, ROBERT DE BORON, in *Joseph* recounts the specifically Christian origin of the Grail, and it is as a Christian relic that it later becomes the subject of its own Arthurian tradition, the principal works of which are WOLFRAM's *Parzival*, the Vulgate *Queste del Saint Graal*, and Book VI of MALORY's *Morte Darthur*. Speculation has arisen, however, concerning the preliterate Grail tradition, the theories being that it has its origin in (1) Celtic vessels of plenty, (2) in the rites of Eastern mystery religions, particularly the Adonis cults, and (3) in early Christian ceremonies, perhaps in the Byzantine Mass. In general, responsible scholarship favors Celtic origin.

Grail Lance. First described by CHRÉTIEN in *Perceval* as part of the GRAIL procession where it bleeds upon the hand of a bearer. PSEUDO-WAUCHIER, however, describes it as standing in a rack and dripping blood into a vessel, and it is then identified with the spear of Longinus with which the side of Christ was pierced. Its Celtic origin probably lies in the spear of LUG which was bathed with blood, and it is almost certainly the same lance with which BAL(A)IN is said to have maimed KING PELLAM by the DOLOROUS STROKE from which he is healed by GALAHAD.

Grail Sword. Presented to PERCEVAL by his host at the GRAIL castle in CHRÉTIEN's *Perceval*. Though it is destined for PERCEVAL, he is informed that it will break under certain circumstances. Later a damsel repeats the warning and sends him in search of a smith, and there the matter ends in CHRÉTIEN. In PSEUDO-WAUCHIER, however, the two parts of the sword are given to GAWAIN and in MANESSIER *Perceval* unites the fragments, though in GERBERT he breaks the sword on the doors of the Earthly Paradise. All of this breaking and mending probably derives ultimately from a Celtic vengeance motif, confused remnants of which reached CHRÉTIEN through the oral tradition.

Grainne. FINN'S young wife who goes off with DIARMAID in the Irish elopement story, *Diarmaid and Grainne*.

Green Knight. Cf. BERCILAK.

Green Knight. English tail-rimed romance (c. 1500) of 516 lines which is apparently a poor redaction of *Sir Gawain and the Green Knight*.

Griffith. In *Historia Meriadoci* murders his brother, CARADOC, King of Wales and father of MERIADOC and ORWEN. He is captured and slain at Mt. Snowdon by ARTHUR and URIEN.

Gringalet, Guingalet. GAWAIN'S horse in CHRÉTIEN'S *Erec* and in Celtic tradition, but not in *Gereint*. In *Escanor*, after GAWAIN wins him, Gringalet will not eat or drink until a bag of powder is put into his ear. A fay later gives him to ESCANOR le Beau. In *Walewein*, WALEWEIN lends him to a squire who wins a trial by combat with him. In the Vulgate *Merlin* GAWAIN takes Gringalet from the Saxon King Clarion. In TRIAD 46A Meingalet and in the BLACK BOOK, Poem VIII, Keincaled is said to be GWALCHEMAI'S spirited horse.

Grisandole. In the Vulgate *Merlin* a princess who disguised as a man captures a wild man whom no man could capture. When the man exposes Caesar's wife as faithless and Grisandole as a princess, Caesar marries Grisandole.

Gryfflet. In MALORY, son of Do of CARDUEL, he is killed by LANCELOT.

Guanhumora. GUINEVERE in GEOFFREY.

Guenloie. In *Yder*, queen whom YDER loves and for whom he seeks to prove his prowess. Possibly the name was a substitute for GUINEVERE since there is an old tradition that YDER loved GUINEVERE.

Guerehes. In the Vulgate *Lancelot* and *Mort Artu*, GAWAIN'S brother killed by BOHORT. Cf. GAHERET.

Guillaume D'Angleterre. French romance attributed by many to CHRÉTIEN retelling the legend of St. Eustace.

Guillaume de Rennes. Usually considered to be the author of *Gesta Regum Britanniae* (c. 1235).

Guillaume le Clerc. Author of *Fergus* (c. 1225).

Guinebaut. In the Vulgate *Merlin*, enchanter brother of BO-HORT and BAN.

Guinevere. ARTHUR'S wife, the daughter of LEODEGAN, and the paramour of LANCELOT. She appears first as GUANHU-MORA in GEOFFREY and in the Welsh legends and TRIADS as Gwenhwyvar (Gvenhvyar) which name TRIAD 56 gives to three women, all "wives of ARTHUR" according to one translation, "great queens of ARTHUR'S court" according to another. She is principally known as the abducted heroine of the MODENA SCULPTURE and CHRÉTIEN'S *Lancelot* where she is carried off by MELEAGANT and rescued by LANCELOT, her lover. She later is kidnapped by MODRED and, in some versions, marries him. She dies a nun. Though as E. K. Chambers' school girl said, she was "very much subject to the misfortune of being run away with," she was apparently regarded as a courtly model by CHRÉTIEN, though writers from MALORY through E. A. Robinson have viewed her as vain and haughty or weak and frivolous. All agree that her illicit and continuing attachment to LANCELOT helps bring on the downfall of ARTHUR'S court. Cf. GWENHWYFAR.

Guinevere, False. In the Vulgate *Merlin*, daughter of LEODEGAN (father of the true Guinevere) and his seneschal's wife. Her relatives try in vain to substitute her as ARTHUR'S bride. In the Vulgate *Lancelot*, she accuses the true Guinevere of taking her place and lures ARTHUR away from court. The Pope puts Britain under an interdict because ARTHUR will not give up the false Guinevere. When both the false Guinevere and her champion, BERTHOLAIS, fall ill, she then confesses to her deceit and ARTHUR returns to the true Guinevere.

Guingalet. See GRINGALET.

Guingambresil. In CHRÉTIEN's *Perceval*, son of King of Cavalon who accuses GAWAIN of killing his father. When GAWAIN does not arrive in time for the duel, Guingambresil postpones it for a year during which period GAWAIN is to bring back the bleeding lance.

Guinglain, Ginglain, Byngalyn. In *Bel Inconnu* or *Guinglain*, the son of GAWAIN who, on the way to free his mistress, the daughter of the King of Wales, from two enchanters, is abused by the damsel Helie.

Guinnion, Fort of. In NENNIUS, the site, still unidentified, of ARTHUR's eighth battle in which ARTHUR carried the image of his Virgin on his shoulders.

Guiron le Courtois. The second part of *Palamedes* which from the thirteenth century on was often given as a separate romance. The first part became *Meliadus*.

Guivret le Petit. In CHRÉTIEN's *Erec* the dwarf king who fights EREC twice (once unwittingly) and then becomes his friend; Gwiffred Petit in *Gereint*.

Gurgalan. In the *Perlesvaus*, the pagan king who gives GAWAIN the GRAIL sword.

Gurnemanz. In WOLFRAM's *Parzival*, educates Parzival in knighthood. He differs from CHRÉTIEN's GORNEMANT in instructing the hero first in religious and ethical matters, then in fighting, and last in courtly love.

Gwair. In Stanza I of *Verses on the Graves* was imprisoned in CAER SIDDI. He is one of the "Three Exalted Prisoners of the Island of Britain" in TRIAD 52. Ynys Wair (Island of Gwair) is Lundy Island and perhaps was regarded as an "Otherworld" island.

Gwalchmei Ap Gwyar. Bearing this Welsh name meaning "hawk (or falcon) of May" GAWAIN appears in the TRIADS where he is not yet associated with ARTHUR. He is mentioned sporadically in Welsh literature: in *Culhwch and Olwen* as the best of Arthur's knights, as the son of ANNA and LLEW AP KYNFARCH and as the son of Gwyar, as the

antagonist of OWEIN, and as an adventurer in *Peredur.*
Cf. GAWAIN.

Gwalhafet. GWALCHMEI's brother in *Culhwch and Olwen.*

Gwasgargerdd Fyrddin in y Bedd (The Song Uttered by Merlin in the Grave). Appears as a prophecy in a manuscript (c. 1300) and in the RED BOOK where MERLIN says he is the son of Morfryn.

Gwawrddur. In the *Gododdin* "glutted black ravens on the rampart of the stronghold though he was not Arthur."

Gwenddolau Ap Ceidio. In *Cyfoesi, Afallennau,* and *Hoianau* MERLIN's sovereign, a chieftain defeated at the battle of ARFDERYDD.

Gwenddydd. In the *Cyfoesi,* MERLIN's sister to whose questions he replies with prophecies. In the *Afallennau* her relationship to MERLIN is not apparent, but he complains that she does not love him or speak to him. She is hostile to him also in the *Hoianau.*

Gwendolen. ARTHUR's wife in the *Historia Meriadoci.*

Gwendoloena. MERLIN's wife in the *Vita Merlini.*

Gwenhwyfach. GUINEVERE's sister in TRIAD 53, "Three Harmful Blows of the Island of Britain."

Gwenhwyfar (Gvenhvyar). Welsh form of GUINEVERE. Two TRIADS (53, "Three Harmful Blows," and 54, "Three Unrestrained Ravagings of Britain") in the RED BOOK refer to MEDRAWT's rough treatment of her and in *Owein* there are "24 maidens more beautiful than GWENHWYFAR." According to Rhy's translation of TRIAD 56, ARTHUR had three wives named GWENHWYFAR. According to other translations the three are queens of ARTHUR's court. In the *Life of St. Gildas,* she is abducted by MELVAS and restored to ARTHUR after the abbot of GLASTONBURY and GILDAS have counselled with him.

Gwgawn. In the *Verses on the Graves,* his grave is mentioned in the same stanza with ARTHUR's.

Gwri Gwallt Earin. Gwri "of the Bright Hair," PRYDERI's name before he is returned to his parents in *Pwyll.*

Gwyar. Father of GWALCHMEI in *Culhwch and Olwen.*

Gwyddawc. In *Culhwch and Olwen*, son of Menestyr. He kills KAY and is killed by ARTHUR to avenge KAY's death.

Gwydre. In *Culhwch and Olwen*, son of ARTHUR, killed in the TWRCH TRWYTH hunt.

Gwyn, Son of Nudd. Appears in a verse dialogue (XXXIII) with Gwyddneu Garanhir in the BLACK BOOK. Here one of the two speakers says, "I have been where Llachau was slain, the son of ARTHUR, extolled in songs." He appears as a huntsman in *Culhwch and Olwen* in whom God put the spirit of the devils of ANNWFN. In the *Life of St. Collen* he is the King of ANNWFN.

Gwynedd. Kingdom in Northwest Wales.

Gwynnhyfar. In the *Vita Gildae* a high officer in ARTHUR's command from CORNWALL and DEVON.

Gwythur. Mentioned in the *Verses on the Graves*, where his grave is noted along with ARTHUR's. In *Culhwch and Olwen*, he is the son of Greidawl who fought with GWYN, son of NUDD, after GWYN abducted Creiddyladl, daughter of Llud.

ↄ

Hartmann von Aue (c. 1170–c. 1210). German poet who wrote *Erek* (c. 1190), the first German Arthurian romance, and *Iwein* (c. 1202). His treatment of the Erec story differs from that of CHRÉTIEN in its emphasis upon morality. He is the first to develop fully the classical German courtly epic.

Hebron. Cf. BRON.

Heinrich von dem Türlîn. Cf. *Crône, Diu.*

Helain. Cf. ELAYNE.

Helie. In *Huth-Merlin*, cited as the author of the *Conte del Brait*. The ascription to him of *Palamedes* in the prologue is considered fraudulent.

Hellekin. Cf. ADAM DE LA HALLE.

Henry of Champagne. Married MARIE, daughter of Louis VII of France and ELEANOR OF AQUITAINE, in 1164.

Henry II of England (1133–1189). Grandson of Henry I, of ANJOU, married ELEANOR OF AQUITAINE, in 1152. According to GIRALDUS, Henry told the monks at GLASTONBURY that he had heard from an old British singer that AR-THUR's body would be found there. It has been suggest-ed that the exhumation of ARTHUR was instigated by Henry in an effort to put an end to the legend of AR-THUR's survival. He was a patron to WACE, commission-ing and then reassigning in 1174 the *Roman de Rou*. It is likely that he was also a patron to THOMAS.

Henry of Huntingdon (1080–1155). In 1139 at Bec in Nor-mandy was shown the "book of Geoffrey Arthur" which he summarized. Later in his *Historia Anglorum* (1129), which covers the period from Julius Caesar to HENRY II, he included an account of ARTHUR based upon GILDAS and NENNIUS between the entries for 527 and 530 in the *Saxon Chronicle*.

Henry of Sully. Abbot at GLASTONBURY when ARTHUR's body was exhumed, according to the history of the abbey by ADAM OF DOMERHAM (c. 1291).

Hereri, Mount. Welsh for Mount Snowdon.

Hermann of Laon. In *De Miraculis S. Mariae Laudunensis* (c. 1146) tells of the visit of nine canons from Laon in Brittany to DEVON and CORNWALL in 1113. In DEVON near Bodmin they were shown ARTHUR's CHAIR and AR-THUR's OVEN. A brawl resulted from a Cornishman's statement that ARTHUR was still alive. Similar fights oc-curred in BRITTANY with the French over ARTHUR's sur-vival.

Hermann von Thüringen (1155–1217). Landgrave, patron of WOLFRAM and other poets such as Walther von der Vogelweide at his court in Eisenach.

Herzeloyde. PARZIVAL'S mother in WOLFRAM'S *Parzival*; GAHMURET'S wife, ANFORTAS' sister, Queen of Wales, ANJOU, and NORGALES. She was won by GAHMURET in a tourney in Wales.

Higden, Ranulph. In *Polychronicon* (c. 1327) questioned the reliability of GEOFFREY based upon the absence of any mention of ARTHUR'S deeds by the Roman, French, and Saxon historians.

Historia Brittonum. Early ninth-century Latin chronicle by NENNIUS, chapter 56 of which tells of ARTHUR, "dux bellorum," and lists his twelve victories: "The first battle was at the mouth of the river called Glein. The second, third, fourth, and fifth were on another river called Dubglas in the region of Linnius. The sixth battle was on the river called Bassas. The seventh battle was in the wood of Celidon; it is Cat Coit Celidon. The eighth battle was on the castle Grunnion, wherein Arthur bore the image of Mary Ever-Virgin on his shoulders .... The ninth battle was fought in the city of the Legion. He fought the tenth battle on the bank of the river called TRIBUIT. The eleventh battle was on the mount called Agned. The twelfth battle was on the mount of Badon, wherein fell 960 men in one day at a single onset of Arthur; and no one overthrew them but he alone, and in all the battles he came out victorious." An attached *Mirabilia* contains the fabulous stories of the grave of ARTHUR'S son, ANIR, and the cairn of ARTHUR'S dog, CABAL.

Historia Meriadoci. Mid-thirteenth-century Latin prose Arthurian romance ascribed to the author of *De Ortu Walwanii.* Meriadoc is the son of the Welsh KING CARADOC who is murdered by his brother GRIFFITH. He is restored to his throne by ARTHUR and URIEN to whom Meriadoc gives his kingdom. Eventually Meriadoc marries the princess of Germany and lives a long, happy life as second in authority to the King of Gaul.

Historia Regum Britanniae (c. 1137). Major work of GEOFFREY OF MONMOUTH. The first report of the *Historia* is that of HENRY OF HUNTINGDON who saw it at the Abbey of Bec in Normandy in 1139. (The Leyden manuscript is known to have been in the library there before 1154 and was probably the one Henry summarized.) Though written as a history of England from its founding by the Trojan Brutus through the reign of the Saxon CADWALLADR and including such well-known stories as those of King Lear and Cymbeline, its chief interest now and in its own day lay in its presentation of the first written account of the whole life of ARTHUR.

Hoel of Cornwall. In *Arthour and Merlin*, Duke of CORNWALL and Duke of TINTAGEL, IGERNE's husband and father of Blasine, Belisent, and Hermesent.

Hoel of Brittany. In GEOFFREY, the imaginary King of BRITTANY who supplies ARTHUR with 15,000 Breton troops.

Hoel of Carhaix. King of BRITTANY, father of ISEULT OF BRITTANY.

Hoianau (Listen, O, Little Pig). In the BLACK BOOK, Poem XVIII, a poem of the Welsh MYRDDIN of 25 stanzas beginning with an address to the piglet, his only companion during the period of his madness in the forest.

Holy Grail. LOVELICH's Middle English alliterative romance (c. 1480) based on the Vulgate *Estoire del Saint Graal*.

Houdenc. Cf. HUSDAIN.

Huchown of the Awle Ryale. Scottish knight to whom the fourteenth-century Alliterative *Morte Arthure* and a number of other metrical romances are attributed.

Hueil. In the *Life of St. Gildas*, eldest brother of GILDAS whom ARTHUR killed.

Hugh de Morville. According to the author of the *Lanzelet* supplied the French book which he translated. He was sent in 1194 to replace Richard Lion-Heart as a hostage in the prison of Leopold of Austria.

Humbaut. Early thirteenth-century incomplete poem (3618 ll.) in which GAWAIN and Humbaut deliver a message from ARTHUR to the King of the Isles but are separated on the return journey.

Huon de Bordeaux. Late twelfth-century verse romance (10,495 ll.) with both Carolingian and Arthurian elements.

Husdain. In BÉROUL'S *Tristan*, TRISTAN's hunting dog who recognizes his master.

Huth-Merlin. Cf. *Suite du Merlin.*

1

Iblis. In *Lanzelet*, daughter of Iweret of Beforet, wife of LANCE-LOT, who remains chaste though LANCELOT marries the Queen of Pluris. Eventually LANCELOT returns to end his days with Iblis at Beforet.

Ider. Cf. *Yder.*

Igerne, Igrayne. Wife of Duke of CORNWALL (GORLOIS in GEOFFREY, HOEL in *Arthour and Merlin*) and mother of ARTHUR. She conceives ARTHUR by UTHER who, with the help of MERLIN's magic, appears to her in the likeness of her husband. After her husband's death, she marries UTHER.

Illtud, St. In the *Life of St. Illtud*, son of Bicanus and Rieingulid, who was received with great honor when he visited his cousin ARTHUR at his court. Illtud had a well-known school at Llanilltud Fawr in Glamorgan, c. 480; GILDAS was his pupil.

Insula Pomorum. Cf. AVALON. In the *Vita Merlini*, the Isle of Apples to which ARTHUR was taken after CAMLANN. Pliny the Elder is the ultimate known source of this description of Elysium, Isidore of Seville the immediate.

Isalie (Ysaye) Le Triste. Fourteenth-century prose romance in which the hero is the son of TRISTAN and ISEULT.

Isdernus. Cf. YDER. On the MODENA SCULPTURE, the second mounted knight following ARTHUR, on the left hand.

Iseult (Ysonde) of Brittany. Sometimes identified as "Iseult of the White Hands," she is wed by TRISTAN because she bears the same name as his beloved ISEULT OF IRELAND, though the marriage is never consummated. Fiercely jealous, Iseult of Brittany tells her mortally wounded husband that ISEULT OF IRELAND is not on the vessel from CORNWALL he has awaited and so causes him to die in despair before his beloved reaches him.

Iseult (Isolt) of Ireland. Irish princess who swears to avenge her father's death at the hands of the Cornish TRISTAN, but who, in some versions of the tale as the result of a potion, falls in love with her enemy and he with her as he escorts her to be the bride of his uncle, KING MARK of CORNWALL. After many intrigues and separations she dies of grief beside her mortally wounded lover.

Isle of Glass. YNYS GUTRIN, British name for GLASTONBURY about 1130. Cf. AVALON.

Ither. PARZIVAL'S kinsman whom PARZIVAL kills, not realizing the seriousness of his action.

Ivain. Cf. *Yvain.*

Ivan (Yvain). In a thirteenth-century poem instructing *jongleurs* in the Matter of Britain by BERTRAN DE PARIS, said to be "the first to tame birds." In the *Jaufre*, Ivan is listed with other characters from CHRÉTIEN.

Iwein. Adapted by HARTMANN VON AUE from CHRÉTIEN'S *Yvain*. HARTMANN'S changes, like those of the *Erek*, emphasize the morality of chivalric conduct.

J

Jacques D'Armagnac. Duc de Nemours for whom a redaction of the VULGATE CYCLE was made by MICHEL GONNOT (C. 1470).

Jaufré. About 1230, Provençal Arthurian verse romance (10,956 ll.). The hero comes to ARTHUR'S court to ask to be knighted in time to be assigned to punish Taulat, who has killed a knight in the presence of the Queen Guilalmer. In the course of his quest Jaufré discovers an underwater fairy land ruled by "la fée du Gibel." Eventually Jaufré fights Taulat and sends him to ARTHUR'S court.

Jeu de la Feuillée. Cf. ADAM DE LA HALLE.

Johfrit de Liez. Knight who instructs LANCELOT in *Lanzelet* as GORNEMANT instructs PERCEVAL in CHRÉTIEN's *Perceval*.

John of Glastonbury. Chronicler of the abbey who at the end of the fourteenth century gave official sanction to the legend of JOSEPH OF ARIMATHEA found in the *Estoire del Saint Graal.*

Joseph d'Arimathie. Verse romance by ROBERT DE BORON (C. 1200) of 3514 lines inspired by CHRÉTIEN's *Perceval*, which recounts for the first time the Christian legend of the GRAIL. Though he asserts that he has as source a book containing the "grant secré" of the GRAIL, the author also states that he is the first to tell its history.

Joseph of Arimathea. Mentioned only briefly in the gospels as a rich follower of Christ who obtained His body from Pilate and had it buried. In Christian legend he is imprisoned by the Jews but is released by the risen Christ who entrusts the GRAIL to him. Later released Joseph forms along with his brother-in-law BRON and some other followers a society of the GRAIL. Eventually BRON's son ALAIN leads the group to GLASTONBURY.

74

Joseph of Arimathea (**English Alliterative**). Fragment of mediocre verse, written before 1375, retelling in simplified form the Vulgate *Estoire del Saint Graal.*

Joseph of Arimathea (**English Prose**). Early sixteenth-century prose retelling of the fourteenth-century alliterative *Joseph of Arimathea.*

Joseph of Exeter. "The only smooth poet" in GEOFFREY's time, to whose aid Milton attributed the excellence of GEOFFREY's Latin verse in Book I of the *Historia.*

Josephé. Son of JOSEPH OF ARIMATHEA, Keeper of the GRAIL, who in the Vulgate *Queste del Saint Graal* comes down from heaven, with his name on his forehead, to celebrate the Mass at the castle of CORBENIC in the presence of GALAAD, PERCEVAL, BOHORT, KING PELLES, and nine other knights.

Josephus, Flavius. (37 A.D.–C. 101). Jewish historian to whom the author of the *Perlesvaus* attributes the "original Latin version."

Joy of the Court. Cf. MABONAGRAIN.

Joyous Gard. In the Vulgate *Lancelot*, the name of the castle of DOLOROUS GARD after LANCELOT captured it and found his name on the lid of the coffin which was to be his. In the Vulgate *Mort Artu*, LANCELOT takes GUINEVERE there after he rescues her from the stake.

K

Kaherdin. Son of KING HOEL, ruler of BRITTANY, brother of ISEULT of BRITTANY who befriends TRISTAN and travels to CORNWALL with him.

Kanelingres. In THOMAS, TRISTAN's father.

Karadoc Brech Bras. See CARADOC BRIEBRAS.

Kardeiz. In WOLFRAM, PERCEVAL's son, LOHENGRIN's twin brother.

Kay (Cai, Cei, Keu). First mentioned in such early Welsh sources as Poem XXXI of the BLACK BOOK, a version of the story of GUINEVERE's abduction in the DIALOGUE OF ARTHUR AND GWENHWYFAR, *Culhwch and Olwen*, and the *Dream of Rhonabwy*. ARTHUR's seneschal, he is from the beginning characterized as a slightly churlish retainer. In later versions, he becomes the son of ECTOR who rears ARTHUR.

Kelliwic. Cf. CELLI WIG.

Keu. Cf. KAY.

Kilhwch and Olwen. Cf. *Culhwch and Olwen.*

King Arthur and King Cornwall. Early sixteenth-century ballad fragment (301 ll.) strongly influenced by the *Pèlerinage de Charlemagne*.

King Arthur's Death. Late fifteenth-century work composed of two poems, the first, a monologue by ARTHUR relating his life story, the second, a summary of the story of the last battle as found in *Morte Arthure* and *Morte Darthur.*

Kyot. From Provence, whose version of the GRAIL story is deemed by WOLFRAM more authentic than that of CHRÉTIEN. His source is cited as a history of the GRAIL by FLEGETANIS. There is doubt as to his existence, and some have identified him as the early thirteenth-century French poet Guiot de Provins. Whether his story of the GRAIL was WOLFRAM's principal source or whether it even existed is, however, a source of controversy.

L

La Bele Garde (La Bele Prise). In the Vulgate *Lancelot* the new name of the DOLOROUS TOWER, CARADO's castle, after LANCELOT kills CARADO.

La Cote Male Tayle (The Ill-Tailored Coat). In MALORY, the name given to BREUNOR by KAY.

Lady of the Fountain. See *Owein.*

Lady of the Lake. There are several, though they shift and merge. (1) The Dame du Lac, a fairy creature who in the Vulgate *Lancelot* rears LANCELOT along with his cousins LIONEL and BOHORT and sends him to ARTHUR's court to be knighted; (2) the Damsel of the Lake (called also NIVIENE, NIMIANE, VIVIANE) who in the VULGATE CYCLE and MALORY beguiles MERLIN by his own enchantments; (3) the Samite-clothed figure in MALORY who gives to and receives from ARTHUR EXCALIBUR; (4) the woman whom BAL(A)IN beheads.

Lady of Malehaut. Cf. GALEHAUT.

Lai du Cor. Late twelfth-century Anglo-Norman poem by Robert Biket about a magic drinking horn which reveals a wife's infidelity. ARTHUR is drenched with wine when he attempts to drink from it but pardons the queen with a kiss when all the others except Garadue (CARADOC) have the same experience. Garadue is awarded the lordship of Cirencester for passing the test.

Lailoken. A fool with prophetic powers at the court of RHYDDERCH HAEL. The legend of his life is the chief source for the *Vita Merlini.*

Lailoken and Kentigern. Scottish story found in a fifteenth-century manuscript describing the confession made by the mad Lailoken to St. Kentigern that he was the cause of the deaths of those who perished at the battle of ARFDERYDD. Lailoken is said in the poem to be thought by some to be MERLIN.

Lailoken and Meldred. Found in the same manuscript with *Lailoken and Kentigern,* relates how the mad Lailoken revealed to King Meldred his wife's infidelity.

Lamorak. In MALORY, PERCEVAL's brother, son of PELLINORE. He is discovered in an affair with MORGAUSE and is killed by GAWAIN.

Lamorat. In the prose *Tristan* PELLINORE'S SON, PERCEVAL'S brother.

Lancelot. In the VULGATE CYCLE and MALORY, the lover of GUIN-EVERE and the "best knight of the world." Though he ultimately derives from the Irish LUG, he first appears in CHRÉTIEN's *Erec* and is the hero of that writer's *Lancelot*, where his adultery with the queen is the *matière*. In fuller histories of the kingdom, we are told that he is the son of KING BAN and QUEEN ELAYNE OF BENWICK who is reared by the DAME DU LAC and comes to ARTHUR's court to be knighted. His love for GUINEVERE having been revealed to ARTHUR by the sons of LOT, he is defeated in the en-suing war and retires to a monastery. The father of GALAHAD, his character embraces the best of the virtues of chivalry as well as its faults.

Lancelot (*Le Chevalier de la Charrette*) (c. 1180). The third of CHRÉTIEN's romances and the first romance to reflect adulterous courtly love. Its *matière* is the abduction of GUINEVERE by MELEAGANT and her subsequent rescue by LANCELOT. LANCELOT has intercourse with her in prison; she is mistakenly accused of relations with her young knights by MELEAGANT; and LANCELOT is trapped in MEL-EAGANT's castle when the poem ends. Its most famous scene is that in which GUINEVERE spurns LANCELOT be-cause he hesitated to ride in a prisoner's cart while on his way to rescue her.

Lancelot (c. 1225). The first branch of the VULGATE CYCLE prop-er, this enormous romance deals with the life of LANCE-LOT up to the GRAIL quest. Its main themes are the hero's rise to the primacy of all ARTHUR's knights, his begetting of GALAHAD, and the preparations for his failure in the GRAIL quest and later tragedy. Taken as a whole the book records its author's gradual disillusionment with chivalry.

Lancelot of the Laik (c. 1482–c. 1500). Incomplete Scottish adap-tation of first section of the Vulgate *Lancelot*.

Lansolet. In a poem (c. 1200) of instruction by Guirant de Calanson to his *jongleur*, the subject of a story to be learned—"Lansolet, how he knew how to conquer Ireland."

Lanval. Late twelfth-century *lai* by MARIE DE FRANCE in which the hero breaks a vow of silence concerning his fairy mistress when GUINEVERE tries to seduce him. After GUINEVERE accuses him of seeking her love and tells of his boast concerning the beauty of his mistress, the fairy comes to ARTHUR's court and all agree that she is the more beautiful.

Lanzelet (c. 1195). German romance by Ulrich von Zatzikhoven which the author says was based on a French book given him by HUGH DE MORVILLE. Unrelated to CHRÉTIEN's *Lancelot*, the poem is a loosely constructed collection of unrelated and largely fantastic adventures.

Laon. Cf. HERMANN OF LAON.

Laudine. In CHRÉTIEN's *Yvain*, the widow of the Knight of the Spring whom YVAIN kills. Married to her with the help of LUNETE Yvain returns to ARTHUR's court but fails to return to her within a year as he had promised. Only after a series of adventures and further trickery on the part of LUNETE, does Laudine accept YVAIN again as her husband.

Launfal. Cf. *Sir Launfal*.

Lausanne (Lake). Lake Geneva, the scene of ARTHUR's victory over the monster cat in the Vulgate *Merlin*.

Layamon (fl. 1200). English priest of Arley Regis in WORCESTERSHIRE, who turned WACE's *Brut* into an English alliterative *Brut* of considerable barbaric force. He states that he used as sources BEDE, the book of "Saints Albin and Augustine," and WACE, though it is clear that the last is his major source. In more than doubling the length of WACE's *Brut*, he transforms WACE's courtly monarch into a warrior king and his romantic chronicle into a tragedy.

Leland, John (1506–52). Chaplain and librarian to Henry VIII,

in his *Itinerarium* recorded his visit about 1535 to GLAS-
TONBURY where he saw ARTHUR's tomb and the lead
cross inscribed "Hic iacet sepultus inclitus rex Arturius
in insula Avalonia" (Here lies buried the famous King
Arthur on the island Avalon). He was also shown the
"bridge called Pontperlus" wherein Arthur cast his
sword. In *Assertio Inclytissimi Arturii* (1544) he described
the seal of ARTHUR in Westminster. He first recorded the
identification of SOUTH CADBURY as CAMELOT.

Leodegan. In the Vulgate *Merlin* King of Carmelide, father of
GUINEVERE and the FALSE GUINEVERE, gives ARTHUR the
ROUND TABLE.

Libeaus Desconus (The Fair Unknown). Early fourteenth-cen-
tury metrical English romance whose hero is GINGLAIN.
THOMAS CHESTRE may have been the author. See also *Bel
Inconnu*, *Wigalois*, and *Carduino*.

Libellus Merlini (c. 1135). Seventh book of GEOFFREY's *Historia*
which had existed as a separate work and which pur-
ported to be a translation of the *Prophécies of Merlin* out
of British into Latin.

Licat Anir. In the *Mirabilia*, a spring near the grave of ARTHUR's
son, ANIR.

Lidel. In *Lailoken and Kentigern*, a place near the field where the
battle of ARFDERYDD was fought. In *Fergus*, the hero
meets GALIENE at the castle of Lidel.

Lidoine. In *Meraugis de Portlesguez*, daughter of the King of
Cavalon. She is the cause of rivalry between MERAUGIS
and GORVAIN CADRUT.

Life of St. Collen. Cf. GWYN.

Life of St. Columba. Cf. ADOMNAN.

Life of St. Efflam. One of two surviving early Breton literary
pieces. It dates from the twelfth century and does not
appear to be dependent on GEOFFREY.

Life of St. Goeznovius. Latin, one of the two surviving early
Breton literary pieces. It mentions ARTHUR's victories,

and apparently is dependent on GEOFFREY, though it is spuriously dated at 1019.

Life of St. Kentigern. Twelfth-century work by Joceline of Furness identifying RHYDDERCH HOEL as a huntsman and a Christian.

Lifric of Llancarfan. Welsh schoolmaster who wrote the *Life of St. Cadoc* (c. 1050) in which ARTHUR appears in unflattering light.

Linnuis. In NENNIUS, region where the second, third, fourth, and fifth battles of ARTHUR were fought on DUBGLAS River. It has been identified as Lindsey in Lincolnshire.

Lionel. In the Vulgate *Lancelot*, BOHORT's brother, LANCELOT's cousin. In the *Queste del Saint Graal* his fury almost leads him to kill BOHORT.

Livre D'Artus. A thirteenth-century continuation of the prose version of ROBERT's *Merlin*. Although its hero is GAWAIN instead of LANCELOT, episodes from the Vulgate *Lancelot* appear.

Livre de Caradoc. Section of the FIRST CONTINUATION (mid-thirteenth-century) of CHRÉTIEN's *Perceval*, adapted from the *Lai du Cor*. CARADOC's wife is here named Guimier, the horn Beneïz or Beneoïz.

Llacheu. Son of ARTHUR appearing in the *Dialogue with Glewlwyd*, in the *Verses on the Graves*, in TRIADS 4 and 91, in the *Spoils of Annwfn*, and in the *Dream of Rhonabwy*. He is unknown to GEOFFREY, but appears as the illegitimate LOHOOT in the French romances.

Llamrei. In *Culhwch and Olwen*, ARTHUR's mare.

Llew Ap Kynfarch. In the Welsh, husband of ARTHUR's sister ANNA and father of GWALCHMEI.

Llongborth. Mentioned in the BLACK BOOK as a battle fought by GEREINT SON OF ERBIN at which ARTHUR's men are said to be bold fighters.

Llwch Llawwynnawg. Appears as one of ARTHUR's warriors in the BLACK BOOK, Poem XXXI, and as ARTHUR's great uncle in *Culhwch and Olwen*. According to one interpretation of *Culhwch and Olwen*, he is ARTHUR'S great uncle on his mother's side.

Llychlyn. In the *Dream of Rhonabwy* country of MARCH, son of Meirchiawn, leader of the troops dressed in white.

Loathly Lady Transformed. Folk motif found reflected in three specifically Arthurian tales—the fifteenth-century romance *The Wedding of Sir Gawain and Dame Ragnell*, Chaucer's *Wife of Bath's Tale*, and a ballad, *The Marriage of Gawain*. In general, all three tell of an elderly hag who rescues a condemned Arthurian knight from death by supplying him with an answer to the question: What do women most desire (sovereignty in marriage)? The motif seems to originate in various Celtic themes, the hero's fitness for the sovereignty over Ireland and the choice of beauty by night or day among others. Its ultimate origin may be in a Celtic sun god myth.

Loc. Father of CHRÉTIEN'S EREC.

Logres. Probably best explained as modern England. Deriving either from Welsh Lloegr or from Locryn, Brutus' successor, it refers to a kingdom south of the Humber and east of the Severn, the land of the English invaders. It is the romantic scene of CHRÉTIEN'S *Lancelot* and *Perceval* and of the VULGATE CYCLE.

Lohengrin (Loherangrin). In WOLFRAM, PERCEVAL'S son who is carried away by a swan when his wife disobeys his command not to question him about his origin.

Lohoot (Loholt, Lohot, Borre, Boarte). Illegitimate son of ARTHUR by LYSANOR. He first appears in *Perlesvaus* where he becomes a knight of the ROUND TABLE and is killed by KAY. In *Lanzelet* he is GUINEVERE'S son. Cf. LLACHEU.

Lot. In the VULGATE CYCLE and MALORY, king of Lothian and Orkney, the husband of ARTHUR'S half-sister, MORGAUSE, who is the mother of GAWAIN, GAHERIS, AGRAVAINE, and MORDRED. One of the recalcitrant British kings, he at first joins ARTHUR's cause, but in MALORY becomes estranged from him after ARTHUR begets MORDRED on MORGAUSE. He is killed by PELLINORE, thus initiating a blood feud between their descendants which erupts finally in the enmity of GAWAIN and LANCELOT which splits the court.

Lovelich, Henry. Translated parts of the Vulgate *Merlin* and the Vulgate *Estoire del Saint Graal* into fifteenth-century English poems of enormous length and dullness.

Lucan. ARTHUR's brother, brother of BEDIVERE, along with GIFLET and ARTHUR only survivors on ARTHUR's side of the battle of CAMLANN in the Vulgate *Mort Artu*.

Luces, Emperor. In WACE and LAYAMON, the Emperor of Rome whom ARTHUR defeats. Cf. LUCIUS HIBERUS.

Luces de Gaut. Name given as author of one version of the prose *Tristan*.

Lucius Hiberus. In GEOFFREY, the Emperor of Rome whom ARTHUR defeats. Cf. LUCES.

Lug (Luch). Irish god whose spear, according to one description, dripped blood and, according to another, was held before a cauldron of blood.

Luin of Celtchar. A magic spear in the Irish sagas.

Lunete. In CHRÉTIEN's *Yvain*, saves YVAIN when he is trapped between two portcullises and convinces her mistress, the widowed LAUDINE, to marry him. Later when YVAIN saves her from the stake she reconciles LAUDINE to him.

Lyones. In MALORY, sister of LYONET, rescued by GARETH whom she later marries.

Lyonet. In MALORY, sister of LYONES, sometimes given the name "Saveage." She fetches GARETH to rescue LYONES.

Lysanor, Lyonors. Daughter of Count Sanam, mother of Borre (LOHOOT), illegitimate son of ARTHUR in MALORY.

⋂

Mabinogion. The title used by Lady Charlotte Guest for her translations (1838–49) of eleven stories from the RED BOOK of Hergest and of the Hanes TALIESIN. She used the term "mabynnogyon," which appears only once and is apparently a scribal error, as a plural of "mabinogi" which was at that time generally misunderstood. "Mabinogi" (the equivalent of *enfance*) should properly be used only for the FOUR BRANCHES: *Pwyll, Branwen, Manawydan,* and *Math,* none of which contain Arthurian material. In addition to the FOUR BRANCHES, however, she included the *Dream of Macsen Wledig, Lludd and Llefelys, Culhwch and Olwen,* the *Dream of Rhonabwy,* the *Lady of the Fountain, Peredur,* and *Gereint Son of Erbin.* The last three romances date from the end of the twelfth century and correspond to CHRÉTIEN's *Yvain, Perceval,* and *Erec et Enide* respectively. *Culhwch and Olwen* (second half of the eleventh century, the earliest Welsh Arthurian piece) and the *Dream of Rhonabwy* (early thirteenth century) are Arthurian, but are unaffected by French romances.

Mabon. In the *Dialogue with Glewlwyd,* one of ARTHUR's men, the "son of Mydron (MODRON), servant of Uthr Pendragon." In *Culhwch and Olwen,* ARTHUR and his men free Mabon from imprisonment at CAER LOYW and Mabon takes the razor from TWRCH TRWYTH. In the *Bel Inconnu,* he is one of the two enchanters who turn the daughter of the King of Wales into a serpent. He is sometimes said to be descended from Apollo Maponos who was worshipped in Gaul and Britain.

Mabonagrain. In CHRÉTIEN's *Erec,* in the episode of the JOY OF THE COURT, the knight who after yielding to EREC explains the secret of the enchanted garden. Some of the

84

elements in the episode correspond to the story of MABON. He does not appear in *Gereint*.

Mabuz. In *Lanzelet*, a magician and the master of the Castle of Death (Schatel le Mort) whom LANCELOT champions against Iweret of Beforet.

Mador de la Porte. In the Vulgate *Mort Artu*, falsely accuses GUINEVERE who had unwittingly given his brother, Gaheries, some poisoned fruit intended for GAWAIN. LANCELOT defeats him and he frees GUINEVERE from her death sentence.

Maelgwn. King of GWYNEDD (died c. 547), one of the kings mentioned by GILDAS.

Maheloas. In CHRÉTIEN'S *Erec*, lord of the winterless ISLE OF GLASS. He is MELWAS of the *Vita Gildae* and MELEAGANT of CHRÉTIEN'S *Lancelot*.

Maid of Astalot. Cf. ASTALOT.

Malduc. In *Lanzelet*, enchanter to whom EREC and GAWAIN surrender in order to persuade him to use his magic to free GUINEVERE imprisoned in a castle surrounded by serpents.

Maledysaunte. In MALORY, the damsel who scolds but helps LA COTE MALE TAYLE in a quest and later marries him and is called Bien Pensaunt and then Beau Vivaunte.

Malory, Sir Thomas. Self-identified author of the fifteenth-century English *Morte Darthur*. Though he refers to himself as a "knight prisoner," his exact identity is disputed. For many years he was thought to be a particular Sir Thomas Malory of Newfold Revell, Warwickshire, who was born in the first quarter of the fifteenth century and died on March 14, 1471, and who indeed spent a great portion of his adult life in prison for a multitude of crimes ranging from extortion to rape. A recent writer, however, identifies him with a Yorkshire knight whose dates more nearly coincide with those of the composition of the *Morte Darthur*. Whatever his identity, his book is the culmination of the medieval Arthurian tradition, the only work to bring together the themes and traditions of chronicle and romance into a single unified work.

Manannan Mac Lin. Irish sea-god, lord of an island "rich in apple-trees."

Manawydan. He is a god of the "Otherworld" and corresponds to the Irish god MANANNAN MAC LIN. Hero of *Manawydan, Son of Llŷr*, one of the FOUR BRANCHES of the *Mabinogion*.

Manawydan. One of the FOUR BRANCHES.

Manessier. In the first quarter of the thirteenth century wrote one of the continuations of CHRÉTIEN's *Perceval* for Countess Jeanne of Flanders. He adds encounters with Satan and the motif of vengeance to the story of a quest to heal the FISHER KING. The GRAIL is seen as a magic vessel of plenty which along with the lance and dish disappears when PERCEVAL dies.

Mannyng, Robert. Translated GEOFFREY or WACE's *Brut* for the first part of his history, *Story of England* (1328).

Manteau Mautaillié (The Poorly-Cut Mantle). Late twelfth-century *lai* or *fabliau*, a chastity test in which a mantle fits perfectly only a chaste woman. The setting is ARTHUR's court and its hero is CARADOC.

Map, Walter (c. 1127–c. 1209). Archdeacon of Oxford in 1197, author of *De Nugis Curialium* and, according to manuscript ascriptions now considered spurious, of parts of the VULGATE CYCLE.

March, Son of Meirchiawn. In the *Dream of Rhonabwy*, leader of the white troops from LLYCHLYN, in the TRIADS (26), owner of the swine DRISTAN guarded, in the *Verses on the Graves* mentioned alongside ARTHUR. Cf. MARK.

Mardol. On the sculpture of the MODENA SCULPTURE, one of the three men defending the fortress.

Mariadok. In THOMAS's *Tristan*, MARK's seneschal.

Marie de Champagne (b. 1145). Daughter of ELEANOR OF AQUITAINE and Louis VII, married Count HENRY of Champagne in 1164. Along with her mother she was a patroness of Courtly Love, and ANDREAS CAPELLANUS, whose *De Amore* is the textbook of Courtly Love, was attached to her court. As patroness of CHRÉTIEN, she commissioned the writing of *Lancelot* (1165) for which the author says she supplied both the *matière* and *sens* (subject matter and meaning).

Marie de France. About 1160 wrote at least 12 rhymed *lais*, two of which have slight connections with ARTHUR, *Lanval* and *Le Chevrefeuil* (*Honeysuckle*). Variously identified, she says of herself only "Marie ai nom, si sui de France."

Mark, King. King of Cornwall, the uncle of TRISTAN and husband of ISEULT. First mentioned as MARCH in the TRIADS, he appears in the first TRISTAN poems, those of THOMAS, EILHART, and BÉROUL in what becomes his traditional character, that of the cowardly, deceived, jealous king. An independent Celtic tradition, however, alluded to only in BÉROUL, maintains that KING MARCH had horse's ears (his name means "horse") and murdered his barbers to conceal his secret.

Marriage of Gawain. Fourteenth-century minor English ballad in which ARTHUR gives GAWAIN without asking him to the LOATHLY LADY to be her husband.

Marrok. In MALORY, "the good knight that was betrayed with his wyff, for she made hym seven yere a warwolff."

Martin of Roecestre. Translated a *Brut* from the Latin according to ROBERT's statement in one of the manuscripts of *Merlin*.

Math, Son of Mathonwy. One of the FOUR BRANCHES.

Medrawt. In the *Annales Cambriae* there is noted in the second entry for 537 "the Battle of Camlann, in which Arthur and Medrawt fell." Two TRIADS (51, 54) tell of Medrawt's attack on ARTHUR's court at CELLI WIG and his abuse of GUINEVERE, and a third (59) refers to the troops of ARTHUR and Medrawt at CAMLANN. Cf. MODRED.

Meigle. In Scotland, claimed to be site of GUINEVERE's grave.

Meleagant. In CHRÉTIEN's *Lancelot*, the abductor of GUINEVERE.

LANCELOT, having crossed a sword bridge, rescues the queen, only to have her whimsically spare Meleagant's life. Subsequently Meleagant kidnaps LANCELOT and accuses GUINEVERE of adultery, but LANCELOT escapes in time to kill Meleagant.

Melehan. In the Vulgate *Mort Artu*, one of MORDRED's sons.

Meliador. French verse romance written (1388–89) by Jean Froissart of Hainaut at the request of Wenceslas, Duke of Luxembourg. The longest (30,771 ll.) of the French Arthurian romances, it deals with Meliador's courtship of the princess of Scotland.

Meliadus. In the prose *Tristan*, the king of Leonois, TRISTAN's father. In *Palamedes*, he is attacked by ARTHUR and others when he carries off the queen of Scotland. His name has sometimes served as the title for the first part of *Palamedes*.

Meliot. In MALORY, NIMIANE's cousin, a party to trapping LANCELOT and GUINEVERE.

Melion. Anonymous *lai* using the story of the werewolf (as in MARIE DE FRANCE's *Bisclavret*) in an Arthurian setting taken largely from WACE.

Mellyagaunce. In MALORY, MELEAGANT.

Melwas. In the *Life of St. Gildas*, the King of the Summer Country who carries off GUINEVERE to GLASTONBURY. When GILDAS intervenes, he returns GUINEVERE to ARTHUR. Cf. MELEAGANT.

Melyon. In LAYAMON, one of MODRED's sons.

Meraugis de Portlesguez. Early thirteenth-century verse romance by Raoul de Houdenc. Following a series of adventures, including a search for GAWAIN and culminating in his defeat of his friend, GORVAIN CADRUT at ARTHUR's court, Meraugis marries Princess LIDOINE and regains the friendship of GORVAIN.

Meriadeuc. Cf. *Chevalier aux Deux Épées*.

Meriadoc. Cf. *Historia Meriadoci*.

Merlin. Magician, prophet, and tutor of the young ARTHUR.

One of the oldest of the Arthurian characters, he derives from the prophet MYRDDIN of the BLACK BOOK, and he has been linked with the naked wild man of the woods, LAILOKEN. He joins the Arthurian story in the three works of GEOFFREY OF MONMOUTH. In GEOFFREY'S *Prophetiae Merlini* (which becomes Book VII of his *Historia*) he is identified with the boy prophet AMBROSIUS (and, says GIRALDUS CAMBRENSIS, with a Scottish Merlin Silvester). In the *Historia* proper, however, he is given a demonic ancestry, and he arranges the conception of ARTHUR by means of a ruse. GEOFFREY'S final work, the *Vita Merlini*, presents his adventures apart from his service to ARTHUR. The romance tradition and the VULGATE CYCLE add the familiar stories of his secreting the infant ARTHUR, his bringing ARTHUR to the throne, and his enchantment by NIMIANE.

Merlin **(English Prose).** A fifteenth-century (c. 1450) translation of the VULGATE CYCLE MERLIN story.

Merlin. Early thirteenth-century poem by ROBERT DE BORON, now extant only as a fragment and in a prose redaction reflected in the VULGATE CYCLE and as an introduction to the *Suite du Merlin*. The story treats in detail MERLIN'S conception by Satan and his involvement with the early history of ARTHUR and has as its major event the establishment of the ROUND TABLE.

Merlin le Sauvage. Late thirteenth-century *lai*, of which only the name survives.

Merveilles de Rigomer. Early thirteenth-century verse romance by Jehan of Cambrai or of Tournai in which LANCELOT and GAWAIN attempt to remove a spell from the castle of Rigomer and deliver its mistress, Dionise.

Mirabilia. Addition to NENNIUS'S *Historia Brittonum* which relates two legends concerning ARTHUR, one concerning the footprint of ARTHUR'S dog CABAL, the other the grave of ARTHUR'S son ANIR.

Modena Sculpture. A sculptured archivolt over the north doorway of the Cathedral of Modena in Lombardy (consecrated 1106) depicting the deliverance of Winlogee (GUINEVERE) from her captors by Artus (ARTHUR) and his knights. The form of the names is Breton. Approaching the center from the left (facing) are three armed mounted knights, the first unnamed, the second with the name Isdernus (YDER) carved above, the third labeled Artus de Bretania. Standing beside the barbican with his ax raised against ARTHUR is Burmaltus (Durmart). Within is Winlogee looking toward ARTHUR, and on the other side of the castle which is in the center stands Mardoc (MARROK) holding a pole. Beyond the barbican rides out Carrado (CARADOC) against the armed mounted knights Galvagin (GAWAIN), Galvarium (GALERON) and Che (KAY).

Modred (Mordred). In MALORY illegitimate son and nephew of ARTHUR by his half-sister MORGAUSE. He is almost certainly derived from MEDRAWT who, according to the *Annales Cambriae*, fell at the Battle of CAMLANN. He is identified by GEOFFREY OF MONMOUTH as a traitor who during ARTHUR's absence usurps the throne and mistreats the queen, a detail first noted in a RED BOOK TRIAD (54), "The Three Unrestrained Ravagings of the Island of Britain." The motif of his incestuous birth appears first in the *Mort Artu* and becomes in MALORY a symbol of the corruption which underlies ARTHUR's court from its conception.

Modron. In *Dialogue with Glewlwyd* and in *Culhwch and Olwen*, the daughter of ABALLACH and mother of MABON. She is an enchanter, and her origins are variously identified in the Irish MORRIGAN, thence perhaps becoming MORGAN LE FAY, or in the Celtic, the goddess Matrona. In TRIAD 70, "The Three Fair Womb-Burdens of the Island of Britain," OWAIN is her son by URIEN. In the *Dream of Rhonabwy* it has been suggested that she and her sisters are "the Flight of Ravens" that always bring victory to OWAIN.

Moise. Cf. MOYSES.

Mongibel. In *Floriant et Florete*, MORGAN's fortress, Mount Aetna, within which ARTHUR lives and awaits the call from Britain.

Mont Dolerous. In GEOFFREY, founded by Ebraucus. In CHRÉTIEN's *Perceval*, identified with the mountain of Melrose in Scotland.

Mont-Saint-Michel. In GEOFFREY, where ARTHUR on his way to Rome fights with and defeats the giant who has seized Helena, the niece of KING HOEL of Brittany.

Morcades. In *Les Enfances Gauvain*, ARTHUR's sister who has a child, Gauvain le Brun, by LOT her page. It is possible that she originated in MORGAN. Cf. MORGAUSE.

Mordrain. In *Estoire del Saint Graal*, the baptismal name of King EVALAC, who is blinded and paralyzed by the GRAIL. He establishes an abbey where later (in the Vulgate *Queste*) GALAHAD heals him.

Mordred. Cf. MODRED.

Morgan le Fay. Wife of URIEN, witch half-sister of ARTHUR, her roots extend deep into Celtic soil. Certainly she is far older than the *Vita Merlini* (c. 1148) in which she makes her first appearance in writing. Her name may derive from that of the Irish war goddess MORRIGAN, or from that of MODRON, daughter of ABALLACH. Whatever her derivation, she is in the VULGATE CYCLE and MALORY a creature of mixed character. She is on the one hand an antagonist of ARTHUR and GUINEVERE, yet she is a healer of Arthurian knights and at the end helps carry ARTHUR to AVALON.

Morgan Tud. In *Gereint*, ARTHUR's physician who heals EREC's wound with a magic medication. The Welsh writer evidently thought Morgan was a man.

Morganis. In GIRALDUS, MORGAN.

Morgause. In MALORY, ARTHUR's half-sister, wife of KING LOT of ORKNEY, mother of GAWAIN and MORDRED. Cf. MORCADES.

Morholt, Morhout, Morold. Brother of the Queen of Ireland, whom TRISTAN kills in order to free CORNWALL from paying tribute.

Morrigan. In Irish legend, battle goddess, an enchanter who assumes the shape of a crow. She may prefigure MORGAN.

Mort Artu (*Didot Perceval*). A portion of the *Didot Perceval*, itself a prose romance existing in two texts, D and E, in manuscripts containing the prose *Joseph* and prose *Merlin* derived from ROBERT DE BORON's poems. In both texts the GRAIL sections are followed by a *Mort Artu* section which treats the final days of the court. A number of theories exist as to the relation of the parts of the *Didot Perceval*, but it seems clear that its compiler was attempting to form an Arthurian tetralogy deriving largely from the work of ROBERT DE BORON consisting of a *Joseph*, a *Merlin*, a *Perceval*, and a *Mort Artu*.

Mort Artu (*Vulgate Cycle*). One of the three original "branches" of the VULGATE CYCLE. A prose romance of great length, the work begins with the return of the GRAIL heroes and closes with the death of LANCELOT. Bringing together in a narrative closely knit by a clear chronology and a careful *entrelacement* such diverse incidents and themes as the "Knight of the Cart," the adultery of LANCELOT and the queen, and the "hope of the Bretons" for ARTHUR's return, the *Mort Artu* is a first step in the process of unification which reaches fruition in MALORY.

Morte Arthur (Stanzaic). Middle English romance (c. 1400) written in dialect of the Northwest Midlands. Derived from the Vulgate *Mort Artu*, the poem begins with LANCELOT's involvement with the MAID OF ASTOLAT and carries the story on to its tragic end. A closely-knit narrative of 3969 lines written in eight-line stanzas, the poem is one of MALORY's sources and an interesting poem in its own right.

Morte Arthure. Fourteenth-century alliterative romance, one of the chief poetic documents of the English Alliterative Revival. Derived principally from WACE, the poet casts his material into the heroic mold of Anglo-Saxon epic poetry and LAYAMON's *Brut*. The poem abounds in spectacular description, notably the description of the giant of St. Michael's mount, the sea battle, and ARTHUR's dream of the wheel of fortune. The poem is variously described as an epic, a tragedy, and a romance, and indeed it has elements of all three.

Morte Darthur. Sir Thomas MALORY's great fifteenth-century work. Long extant only in CAXTON's edition of 1485 and generally regarded, as CAXTON regarded it, as the first work to bring together into a single unified history all the diverse elements of the ARTHUR story, the discovery of a manuscript copy of the *Morte Darthur*, both earlier and fuller than CAXTON's edition, led to speculation that MALORY intended to write not a single unified work, but eight separate romances on Arthurian themes. Whatever his intentions, MALORY, working principally from the VULGATE CYCLE in an increasingly inventive fashion, did compile the most complete Arthurian work in any language and one of the masterpieces of English literature.

Mount Aetna. Cf. MONGIBEL and GERVASE OF TILBURY.

Mount Badon (*Mons Badonicus*). Last of ARTHUR's twelve great victories against the Saxons, first mentioned by GILDAS. The chief candidates for the site are BATH, Badbury Rings in Dorset, and Liddington Castle in Wiltshire.

Mount Breguoin. Appears in the Vatican recension (944) in place of NENNIUS's MONS AGNED. It is possibly High Rochester in the Cheviots, the site of one of the twelve victories of ARTHUR noted by NENNIUS.

Moyses. In ROBERT DE BORON's *Joseph d'Arimathie*, is swallowed up by the earth when he attempts to sit in the chair reserved at the GRAIL table for BRON's unborn descendant.

Mule Sans Frein (*Mule without a Bridle*). Early thirteenth-century verse romance by Paien de Maisières (which recounts the adventures of KAY and GAWAIN in recovering the bridle of a maiden's mule.

Myrddin. In the *Afallenau*, and in *Hoianau*, laments in his madness his miserable state after the battle of ARFDERDYDD in which he lost his lord, GWENDDOLAU, and won the hatred of RHYDDERCH and GWENDDYDD. In GEOFFREY's *Vita Merlini* GWENDDYDD (Ganieda in Latin) is Myrddin's sister. In the *Cyfoesi* Myrddin has prophetic powers. He has been identified with another wild man of the woods, LAILOKEN, who lived at the court of King Rederech and prophesied his death. He corresponds to the Irish SUIBNE GEILT and becomes MERLIN in GEOFFREY.

N

Nascien. In *Estoire del Saint Graal*, baptismal name of Seraphe, the brother-in-law of KING EVALAK, father of CELIDOINE. Stricken with blindness when curiosity leads him to uncover the GRAIL, he is healed by the bleeding lance. Along with MODRAIN and CELIDOINE, he joins JOSEPH and JOSEPHÉ in converting Britain to Christianity. GALAHAD is the last of his lineage.

Nennius. Early ninth-century chronicler of the *Historia Brittonum* which contains the first mention of ARTHUR as the victor at MOUNT BADON, the last of 12 victories over the Saxons, in which he is said to have slain 960 of the enemy. Nennius also mentions the miracles of the graves of ANIR, ARTHUR's son and of CABAL, ARTHUR's dog. His work is largely a compilation of earlier documents and of oral tradition.

Nentres. King of Garlot (Nantres de Gurelot in the French romances); in MALORY, the husband of ARTHUR's half-sister, ELAYNE.

Nimiane, Niniane, Niviene. Cf. LADY OF THE LAKE.

Norgales. North Wales.

Nudd. Descended from the British god Nodons, in *Culhwch and Olwen*, King of ANNWFN, father of GWYN, who fights every May day until Domesday with GWYTHYR for the hand of Creiddylad; in the *Dream of Rhonabwy*, the father of EDERN, who is the leader of the black troops from Denmark.

Nyneve. Cf. LADY OF THE LAKE.

O

Octha. In NENNIUS, a Saxon, the son of Hengist, who settled in Kent and fought against ARTHUR.

Ocvran. Variant of GOGRVAN, father of GUINEVERE in Welsh literature.

Oeth. Appears in the *Verse on the Graves*, the TRIADS (in 52, *Caer Oeth and Anoeth*), and *Culhwch and Olwen* as a place or castle of wonders or difficulties.

Olwen. In *Culhwch and Olwen*, daughter of the giant YSBADDADEN. CULHWCH, having been fated by his step-mother to love only Olwen, performs the tasks set by her father and marries her.

Orcanie. A form of ORKNEY, in CHRÉTIEN's *Perceval*, the site of ARTHUR's court.

Ordericus Vitalis. In his *Historia Ecclesiastica* (1134) excerpts sections from GEOFFREY's *Prophetiae Merlini*.

Orguelleuse de Logres, Orgeluse. In CHRÉTIEN's *Perceval*, a haughty lady who insults GAWAIN. In *Parzival*, scorned by PARZIVAL because of his marital fidelity, she falls in love with GAWAIN who proves himself worthy of her.

Orguelleus de Limors, Count. In CHRÉTIEN's *Erec*, after EREC is apparently dead, forces ENIDE to become his wife. After the marriage ceremony when ENIDE refuses to eat or drink, he slaps her and the sound of the slap arouses EREC, who then kills the count.

Orkney. Kingdom inherited by GAWAIN from his father, LOT.

Osla. In the *Dream of Rhonabwy*, ARTHUR's opponent in the battle of MOUNT BADON. He sends an embassy to ARTHUR to seek a truce.

Otranto, Cathedral of. Site of a mosaic pavement (1166) depicting ARTHUR (*Arturus Rex*) riding a goat.

Owain. Son of URIEN of RHEGED by MODRON, sixth-century North British hero in the wars against the Angles. The *Book of Taliesin* describes his battles with MABON over the cattle of URIEN and laments his death at the hand of Flamdwyn (though in one translation Owain kills Flamdwyn!). His major appearance, however, is in the *Dream of Rhonabwy* where he plays a game of *gwyddbwyll* with ARTHUR. In the course of the game ARTHUR and Owain attempt to control an offstage battle between Owain's ravens and ARTHUR's squires. As Owein he is the hero of the *Lady of the Fountain*. Cf. YVAIN.

Owein (Lady of the Fountain). Middle Welsh prose romance contained in the RED BOOK and the WHITE BOOK, selected by Lady Charlotte Guest for inclusion in the *Mabinogion*. It is the Welsh counterpart of CHRÉTIEN's *Yvain*, with which it probably shares a common source, and differs from it only in minor details, some of which are distinctly Welsh in origin.

P

Padarn, St. In *Vita Paterni* (twelfth century), caused the earth to swallow up (*absorbet*) ARTHUR when ARTHUR demands his tunic.

Paien de Maisières. Author of *Mule Sans Frein*.

Palamedes. In the prose *Tristan*, ISEULT's faithful Saracen knight who loves her. In MALORY he also follows the BESTE GLATISSANT and is eventually made Duke of Provynce by LANCELOT.

Palamedes. French prose romance containing the *Meliadus* and the *Guiron le Courtois*, which have since the thirteenth century been presented as separate romances. The work is ascribed, probably falsely, to HELIE, companion of ROBERT DE BORON. In the story, MELIADUS, King of Leonois and father of TRISTAN, is a poet and musician who carries off the Queen of Scotland with whom he has been having an affair. ARTHUR and MELIADUS's other enemies join in fighting him until Guiron le Courtois, the hero of the rest of the poem, puts an end to the war.

Palug's Cat. Cf. CATH PALUG.

Pant. In *Lanzelet*, King of GENNEWIS and father of LANCELOT by Clarine. He dies while fleeing with his wife and son from the revolt in GENNEWIS.

Parzival. Cf. WOLFRAM VON ESCHENBACH.

Pellam. The Maimed King, father of PELLES. In the *Suite du Merlin* he is wounded by the DOLOROUS STROKE struck by BAL(A)IN and eventually cured by GALAHAD, his great-grandson. He may have come into being through a confusion with PELLINORE and later assumed a separate role.

Pellean, Pellehen. PERCEVAL's father in the Vulgate *Queste* (Pellehen), in the *Suite du Merlin* (Pellean), and in the Portuguese *Demanda* (Pellean). Cf. PELLINORE.

Pelles. Along with PELLAM and Aleyn, one of the FISHER KINGS, possibly the original. His name may derive from Cornish *peller*, "wise man," and it has been conjectured that he first appears as PWYLL in the *Mabinogion*, though there are other theories. He is wounded in the thigh as punishment for drawing the Sword of David, though there is some confusion here with PELLAM his father and PELLINORE his brother. In the Vulgate *Lancelot*, he is the father of ELAYNE, mother of GALAHAD.

Pellinore. The King of the Isles. He is the brother of PELLES and father of LAMORAK and PERCEVAL (See PELLEAN). In the romances he follows the BESTE GLATISSANT (see PALAMEDES) and like PELLES his brother he is wounded through the thigh. Though MALORY confuses him with PELLAM, his killing of KING LOT in battle and his own death at the hands of GAWAIN and his brothers brings on the feud that eventually splits the ROUND TABLE.

Perceforest. Fourteenth-century prose romance, a vast compilation of ALEXANDER stories combined with themes of the GRAIL.

Perceval. The original GRAIL hero. In CHRÉTIEN'S *Perceval* or *Conte del Graal* the only surviving son of a widow, he determines to become a knight and journeys to ARTHUR'S court where he is tutored by GORNEMANT who warns him against loquacity. On his first adventure he is directed to a strange castle where he witnesses a procession in which is carried among other things a *graal* or platter. Later he learns that had he inquired concerning the *graal*, the surrounding land, now wasted, would have been made fertile and its king, now maimed, whom he had observed fishing been made whole. He is then told that his mother has died from grief. He is cursed for his callousness on both counts and later wanders about searching for the GRAIL castle and eventually learns that the FISHER KING is his cousin. In the prose *Joseph* and prose *Merlin* he becomes the son of ALAIN, son of BRON, and having been cursed for attempting to sit in the PERILOUS SEAT goes searching for the GRAIL (now the Christian vessel) which he eventually finds and by asking the proper questions cures the FISHER KING. In the *Perlesvaus* Britain is the Waste Land and PERCEVAL must, after a hazardous quest, cure ARTHUR among others. In the fourteenth-century *Sir Perceval of Galles* he is reduced to burning witches and killing giants and in MALORY he is simply an extra GRAIL knight, included, one feels, out of deference to his tradition.

Perceval. Romance of CHRÉTIEN DE TROYES. Written c. 1181 at the request of PHILIPPE OF ALSACE who, he says, gave him the book. The poem deals with the GRAIL adventures of PERCEVAL and GAWAIN. It is unfinished, possibly because of CHRÉTIEN's death, and so its symbols, particularly the GRAIL, and its ultimate meaning remain unclear.

Perceval, First Continuation. Sometimes called the *Pseudo-Wauchier* and the *Gawain Continuation*, a six-section addition to CHRÉTIEN's poem, four of which deal with adventures of GAWAIN, including a visit to the GRAIL castle. The eleven manuscripts containing the work bear witness to three redactions ranging from 9500 to 9600 verses of which the shortest version is thought to be the oldest. The section of the work dealing with CARADOC is often considered to be a separate work, the *Livre de Caradoc*.

Perceval, Second Continuation. A 13,000 line continuation of the FIRST CONTINUATION, sometimes called the *Perceval Continuation*. Though PERCEVAL here visits the GRAIL castle and mends the broken GRAIL SWORD, the poem is obviously unfinished.

Perceval's Aunt. In the Vulgate *Queste*, at one time the queen of the Terre Gastee, tells PERCEVAL of his mother's death and of the GRAIL table and the ROUND TABLE and warns him that he can achieve the GRAIL only if he is chaste.

Perceval's Sister. In the Vulgate *Queste* replaces the hangings on David's sword with her hair, tells the story of the DOLOROUS STROKE, and girds the sword on GALAHAD. Later her dead body is found on Solomon's ship, in her hand a scroll relating her life and death.

Peredur, Son of Eliffer. One of the seven sons of Eliffer, a northern ruler. The *Annales Cambriae* lists for the year

580 the death of Peredur and his brother Gwrgi at the battle of ARFDERYDD. Neither of these is mentioned in the early Welsh poetry, but he is obviously the PEREDU- RUS in GEOFFREY and the hero of the Welsh tale although his father there is said to be Efrawg. In the *Verses on the Graves*, the grave of Mor, the son of Peredur Penwedig (Chief Physician) is described.

Peredur. Early thirteenth-century Welsh tale, most complete text of which is found in the WHITE BOOK, which corresponds to CHRÉTIEN's *Perceval*. Of the three tales contained in the MABINOGION, *Peredur* differs the most from the corresponding romances of CHRÉTIEN and is thus possibly older than the other two, having gone through more redactions.

Peredurus. In GEOFFREY's *Vita Merlini*, the king of North Wales who with Rodarchus, King of Cumberland, wages a war with Guennolous, King of Scotland.

Perilous Bed. In CHRÉTIEN's *Perceval*, on which GAWAIN sits, thus causing bells to ring, windows to open, and arrows and bolts to pierce his armour and his body. In the Vulgate *Lancelot*, LANCELOT survives a Perilous Bed in a castle near MELEAGANT's land, where a flaming lance is thrown at him.

Perilous Seat. In the Vulgate *Queste* and in MALORY occupied by GALAHAD. In ROBERT's *Merlin* it is called the Empty Seat.

Perlesvaus. Early thirteenth-century prose romance in which GAWAIN, LANCELOT, and Perlesvaus go on a quest for the GRAIL. Only Perlesvaus is successful and rescues the GRAIL castle from the king of CASTLE MORTAL. The author's emphasis is upon Christian knighthood rather than upon courtly love and adultery and though he cites JOSEPHUS as his source, it is obvious that he relies upon CHRÉTIEN and ROBERT DE BORON.

Peter des Roches. Bishop of Winchester, said in the *Lanercost Chronicle* to have dined with KING ARTHUR in 1216.

Peter of Blois. Breton writer who in *De Confessione* (c. 1190) noted that *histriones* (*conteurs*) tell stories about ARTHUR, GAWAIN, and TRISTAN which move their audience to tears and that, like the Jews, the Bretons await the return of their saviour.

Petit Cru. In THOMAS, the dog which TRISTAN sends to ISEULT to comfort her with the music of its bell while they are apart. ISEULT by breaking the bell insures that she will not be happy while TRISTAN is away.

Petrus. In ROBERT's *Joseph*, one of JOSEPH's disciples who goes with BRON and ALAIN "westward" (evidently to GLASTONBURY) with the GRAIL.

Philippe of Alsace (c. 1143–91). Made Count of Flanders in 1168, married MARIE DE CHAMPAGNE in 1164, made Regent of France (1180–1182), died at Acre on the Third Crusade. For a time he was CHRÉTIEN's patron and according to the *Perceval*, which CHRÉTIEN dedicated to him in an exaggerated encomium, gave CHRÉTIEN the book to be translated.

Philomena. Poem (possibly twelfth-century) included in the late thirteenth-century *Ovide Moralisé* and attributed by the compiler to CHRÉTIEN's *Le Gois*. In the beginning of *Cligès* CHRÉTIEN listed among his works the episode of Philomela and Procne from Ovid's *Metamorphoses*.

Post-Vulgate *Mort Artu*. Cf. VULGATE CYCLE.

Post-Vulgate *Queste*. Cf. VULGATE CYCLE.

Powys. Kingdom of Northeastern Wales.

Preiddeu Annwfn. Cf. *Spoils of Annwfn*.

Prester John. In WOLFRAM's *Parzival*, son of FEIREFIZ and the GRAIL bearer, his wife, Repanse de Schoye. In the Middle Ages he was thought to be a fabulously rich king and priest of a vast kingdom in Asia or Africa. Although he was likely mythical from the beginning, popes tried to communicate with him for hundreds of years.

Pridwen, Prydwenn. In the *Spoils of Annwfn* and *Culhwch and*

Olwen, ARTHUR'S ship; in GEOFFREY'S *Historia*, ARTHUR'S shield.

Prophécies de Merlin. Prose romance translated from Latin by Richard of Ireland for the Emperor FREDERICK II of Sicily in the 1270's using various French Arthurian romances and featuring actual events which Merlin "prophesies." Evidently the authorship, source, and patron are as fictitious as the *ex post facto* prophecies.

Prophecy of the Eagle. Quoted by GIRALDUS, contains eight of the prophecies of MERLIN Silvester.

Prophetiae Merlini. Written by GEOFFREY about 1135 and later incorporated into the *Historia* with additional prophecies and other information about the character. GEOFFREY identifies NENNIUS'S AMBROSIUS and the Welsh prophet MYRDDIN with MERLIN, grandson of the king of DYFED.

Prose *Lancelot*. Cf. VULGATE CYCLE.

Prose *Tristan*. Cf. VULGATE CYCLE.

Prydein. Britain in Welsh.

Pryderi. In *Pwyll*, the name of GWRI GWALLT-EURYN after he is returned to his parents, PWYLL and Rhiannon. In *Manawydan* he becomes the stepson of MANAWYDAN and both brings a curse upon the country and frees it from the curse. He appears with PWYLL in the *Spoils of Annwfn* saying that the prison of Gweir was well-equipped. This "Otherworld" divinity may have evolved into PERCEVAL.

Pseudo-Robert de Boron Cycle. Cf. VULGATE CYCLE.

Pseudo-Wauchier. Cf. *Perceval*, FIRST CONTINUATION.

Pucci, Antonio. Cf. CARDUINO.

Pwyll. Prince of DYFED in the first Branch of the *Mabinogion*. He may have evolved into PELLES.

Pwyll. The first branch in the *Mabinogion* which tells of the exchange between ARAWN, "Otherworld" king and PWYLL, in which PWYLL takes ARAWN'S appearance and place but does not sleep with his wife.

Q

Queste del Saint Graal. Dated between 1215–1230, the section of the VULGATE CYCLE dealing with the quest for the GRAIL after it mysteriously appears and serves the knights of the ROUND TABLE. Its hero is GALAHAD to whom at CORBENIC Castle the GRAIL appears together with the bleeding lance with which the hero heals the Maimed King. BOHORT, PERCEVAL, and GALAHAD are then transported to the Land of SARRAS where GALAHAD dies.

R

Raoul. Cf. *Vengeance Raguidel.*

Raoul de Houdenc. Cf. *Meraugis.*

Red Book of Hergest. One of *Four Ancient Books of Wales,* a late fourteenth-century Welsh manuscript found at Jesus College, Oxford, which contains: the *Mabinogion (Pwyll, Branwen, Manawyddan, Math), Macsen's Dream, Lludd and Llevelys, Culhwch and Olwen,* the *Dream of Rhonabwy, Owein and Lunet, Peredur, Gereint and Enid,* and some *Triads.* It is also an important Welsh chronicle and contains the corpus of Welsh court poetry.

Renaud de Beaujeu. Cf. *Bel Inconnu.*

Rheged. Seventh-century British kingdom extending from the Scottish border to Lancashire.

Rhydderch Hael (RHYDDERCH THE GENEROUS, RODARCHUS LARGUS in GEOFFREY). In the *Afallennau,* defeated MYRDDIN's lord, GWENDDOLAU, at the battle of ARFDERYDD, and MYRDDIN speaks bitterly of him in the *Hoianau*. He is identified as Rhydderch ap Tudwal, late sixth-century king of Dumbarton. In *The Thirteen Treasures of the Isle of Britain* he is said to have a *dysgyl*, a magic vessel which provides whatever food one wishes.

Rion. King of Ireland in LAYAMON and MALORY represented as a pagan giant.

Rivalen. Name of TRISTAN's father after the legend entered Breton tradition; historically, the father of Tristan of Vitré c. 1030.

Robert de Boron. Late twelfth-century poet who wrote *Joseph d'Arimathie* and *Merlin* in which the GRAIL, the chalice of the Last Supper, is brought to Britain.

Robert de Chesney. Bishop of Lincoln, to whom GEOFFREY dedicated the *Vita Merlini*.

Robert, Earl of Gloucester. Supporter of Matilda, daughter and heir to King Henry I, to whom GEOFFREY at one time dedicated the *Historia*.

Robert of Gloucester. Fourteenth-century chronicler whose history of Britain relies heavily on GEOFFREY.

Robert of Torigni. Twelfth-century abbot of MONT-SAINT-MICHEL to whom the biographical romances *Historia Meriadoci* and *De Ortu Walwanii* were once falsely ascribed.

Roman de Rou. Chronicle of the Norman Kings (begun c. 1160) by WACE in which the magic fountain in the forest of BROCELIANDE is described.

Roman du Graal. Fanni Bogdanow's term for a long, unified post-VULGATE CYCLE of romances containing the *Estoire del Saint Graal*, the prose redaction of ROBERT DE BORON's *Merlin*, the *Suite* and post-Vulgate versions of the *Queste* and *Mort Artu*.

Round Table. First mentioned by WACE as a device to prevent quarrels among the knights as to seating precedence. Since a similar passage not derived from WACE occurs in LAYAMON, it has been reasoned that both derive independently from lost Welsh accounts of table brawling to which Irish parallels exist. Other scholars derive the famous board from Celtic May-day ring tables or from "turning tables." MALORY, reflecting the French romance tradition, notes two origins: that the Round Table was a part of GUINEVERE's dowry and that "Merlyon made the Rounde Table in tokenyng of rowndnes of the worlde, for men sholde by the Rounde Table understonde the rowndenes signyfyed by ryght." Interestingly also, the Round Table has sometimes been thought to refer to such enclosures as that at SOUTH CADBURY.

Also an entertainment including jousting, feasting, dancing, and an imitation of the Round Table with impersonations of the knights popular in England and on the continent during the thirteenth and fourteenth centuries.

Rusticiano da Pisa. Compiled for KING EDWARD I of England around 1270 a group of adventures beginning with an account of Branor le Brun, a 120 year-old knight of the ROUND TABLE. Generally he is identified as the Rusticiano da Pisa who in 1298 wrote a French account of Marco Polo while they were both in prison in Genoa.

S

Sagremor. In CHRÉTIEN's *Perceval*, along with KAY, interrupts PERCEVAL in his reverie on the three drops of blood in the snow. In the *Queste del Saint Graal* he, ARTHUR, and YVAIN are predicted to be slain by MORDRED, and in the prose *Tristan* he brings the dying TRISTAN his sword and shield. In his most romantic appearance, in *Meliador* he declares his love for SÉBILLE and is sustained through his adventures by her parting glance.

Salisbury Plain. Sometimes identified as the general area of the battle of MOUNT BADON, in the Vulgate *Mort Artu* the scene of the final battle between ARTHUR and MORDRED.

Sarras. In the Vulgate *Queste*, the imaginary land of the Saracens where GALAHAD, BOHORT, and PERCEVAL are taken in Solomon's ship and where GALAHAD dies in ecstasy after seeing the mystery of the GRAIL.

Sébille. In the *Prophécies de Merlin*, a fay; in *Meliador* the ingenue object of SAGREMOR's love.

Second Continuation. Cf. PERCEVAL, SECOND CONTINUATION.

Segontium. Roman fort near CAERNARVON, SINADON in *Bel Inconnu*.

Segremors. German poem modelled on *Meraugis de Portlesguez*.

Seifrid de Ardemont. A late thirteenth-century romance by ALBRECHT VON SCHARFENBERG relying heavily upon WOLFRAM's *Parzival*.

Senchus Fer nAlban. List of Pictish kings in which ARTHUR is listed as the grandson, not the son, of AEDAN.

Sigune. In WOLFRAM's *Parzival*, PARZIVAL's cousin who curses him when she learns that he failed to ask the proper questions at the GRAIL castle. She also tells PARZIVAL who he is.

Sinadon. In *Bel Inconnu*, the ruined city, the site of the episode of the dragon kiss.

Sir Gawain and the Green Knight. Fourteenth-century romance by the author of *Pearl*, *Purity*, and *Patience*. A skillful fusing of two Celtic motifs—The Champion's Bargain and the Temptation—the poem deals with the testing of GAWAIN who, having undertaken to receive a blow at the hands of the enchanted GREEN KNIGHT, resists the overtures of his host's wife only to fall prey to the temptation to save his own skin. The poem, one of the acknowledged masterpieces of English literature, presents, in spite of its many problems of interpretation, a beautifully structured and varied tale of knightly adventure.

Sir Launfal (c. 1340). English rimed romance by THOMAS CHES-

TRE influenced by MARIE DE FRANCE'S *Lanval* and *Grae-lent.* The Fairy Mistress motif is subordinated to chivalric themes.

Sir Perceval of Galles. Middle English rimed romance (c. 1340) in which the GRAIL does not appear. A crudely constructed and written piece, the poem delights in the grotesque rather than the holy and is filled with marvels which seem at times deliberately ludicrous.

Sir Tristrem. Middle English (c. 1300) rimed romance based on THOMAS'S *Tristan.* Utilizing an awkward eleven-line stanza made up of two and three-stress lines, the poem shows none of the charm or fervor of its courtly original.

Sone de Nausay. Late thirteenth-century romance on the GRAIL legend in which JOSEPH OF ARIMATHEA is the FISHER KING.

Soredamors. in CHRÉTIEN'S *Cligès* GAWAIN'S sister who marries ALEXANDRE, son of the Emperor of Constantinople, and becomes the mother of CLIGÈS.

South Cadbury Castle. Standing on a hill near the Somerset-Dorset border, a hillfort fortified from Neolithic times and associated with ARTHUR since at least the sixteenth century. Locally identified as CAMELOT probably because of the close proximity of the villages of Queen Camel and West Camel, both named for the local river, the Cam or Camel. Whatever its precise relation to ARTHUR, it was almost surely the "court" of a strong early sixth-century British warlord.

Sovereignty of Ireland (Sovranty of Erin). In the Irish adventure, *The Prophetic Ecstasy of the Phantom,* LUG'S wife who, like the GRAIL maiden, provides food and changes into a LOATHLY LADY.

Spoils of Annwfn. Poem XXX in the BOOK OF TALIESIN. It recounts an expedition of ARTHUR in his ship PRYDWENN to ANNWFN, the Celtic "Otherworld," to get the magic cauldron of the chief of ANNWFN.

Stricker, Der. Author of *Daniel vom Blühenden Tal.*

Suibne Geilt. Latter half seventh-century legendary king of Dâl nAraide who went mad in the battle of Moira. He is Irish counterpart of MERLIN.

Suite du Merlin (Huth Merlin). Continuation, based in part upon the Vulgate *Merlin*, of a prose redaction of ROBERT DE BORON'S *Merlin*. It was formerly called the Huth Merlin because it existed only in the manuscript British Museum Addium 38117 which had belonged to the Huth family. Since a fragment of the romance has been found in another manuscript, the name *Suite du Merlin* is now generally used.

Sword in the Stone. The tradition, originating in the Vulgate *Merlin*, that ARTHUR drew a magical sword from a stone in order to prove his kingship. In the Vulgate *Queste*, a similar sword is drawn from a stone by GALAHAD to be used by him in the GRAIL quest.

Taliesin. Sixth-century composer of panegyrics of, among ARTHUR'S warriors, URIEN of RHEGED, and OWAIN. It is uncertain which of the poems in the BOOK OF TALIESIN are actually his. In NENNIUS and GEOFFREY he is called Thelgisinus.

Terre Foraine. In the *Estoire del Saint Graal* a kingdom whose leper king is healed and converted by ALAIN. In the Vulgate *Lancelot* the kingdom of BAUDEMAGUS, the father of MELEAGANT, where GUINEVERE is held captive.

Thomas of Britain. In the second half of the twelfth century wrote an Anglo-Norman verse *Tristan*, probably at the court of HENRY II. About 3150 lines of his poem have survived in fragments. One of his most interesting additions to the TRISTAN legend was the creation of the hidden underground shrine in which TRISTAN kept an image of ISEULT.

Tintagel. Picturesque ruin on a Cornish peninsula identified as the castle of IGERNE, the mother of ARTHUR, in GEOFFREY and as MARK's stronghold in BÉROUL. In CHRÉTIEN's *Perceval*, GAWAIN goes to Tintagel and takes part in a tourney to please the Maid of the Little Sleeves, daughter of Tiebaut of Tintagel.

Tor. In MALORY, the son of PELLINORE by the wife of Aryes the cowherd. He is killed by LANCELOT in his ill-fated abduction of GUINEVERE.

Tortain. In the FIRST CONTINUATION of *Perceval*, a boar (TWRCH TRWYTH), son of Heliares.

Trevrizent. In WOLFRAM's *Parzival*, PARZIVAL's hermit uncle whose name is usually given to Book IX. He instructs PARZIVAL in Christian theology and the secrets of the GRAIL, which here is a stone, *lapis exillis* (scribal error perhaps for *lapis exilis*, worthless stone), possibly a symbol of humility. After two weeks, Trevrizent absolves PARZIVAL of his sins.

Triads, Welsh. Collections of short items—moral, gnomic, proverbial, historical, legal, etc.—having a common attribute and arranged in groups of three, e.g., "Three Battle-Horsemen of the Island of Britain" or "Three Gate-Keepers at the Action of Bangor Orchard." Some 96 taken principally from the *Four Ancient Books* deal with the Island of Britain and contain numerous references to ARTHUR, CAMLANN, etc. These are thought to be mnemonic devices for the training of bards and date well before the time of GEOFFREY OF MONMOUTH.

Tribruit, Tryfrwyd. In NENNIUS, the river on whose shore ARTHUR's tenth battle was fought. Along with MOUNT BADON it is mentioned in a later Arthurian legend. In the *Dialogue with Glewlwyd Gafaelfawr*, BEDWYR fights on the strand of the Tryfrwyd.

Tristan. Cornish knight whose history comes to be associated with ARTHUR'S court. One of the TRIADS (26) associates a DRYSTAN (a name of probable Pictish origin) with "March," as does perhaps the TRISTAN STONE, and even earlier (1160) he is mentioned as a lover by the Provençal poet, Bernart de Ventadorn. MARIE DE FRANCE'S *Lai du Chèvrefeuil* assumes an already existing Tristan-Iseult story, though it does not place the hero in ARTHUR'S court. By 1160 the Tristan legend was connected with ARTHUR. THOMAS wrote a complete version of the legend in Anglo-Norman verse, little of which survives. GOTTFRIED VON STRASSBURG, EILHARDT VON OBERG, and BÉROUL all present a more or less consistent version of the story in which are related TRISTAN'S assignment to convey to CORNWALL his Uncle MARK'S betrothed, the Irish princess ISEULT, their drinking of the love potion, their clandestine meetings, and their final tragedy.

Tristan als Mönch (Tristan as a Monk). Late thirteenth century Alsatian poem based upon the incident in which TRISTAN, disguised as a monk, catches ISEULT when she trips coming from a boat on her way to be tested for fidelity. ISEULT can thus swear that she has never been in the arms of any man other than her husband, except of course, the monk. The poem is included in some manuscripts as a continuation of GOTTFRIED'S *Tristan*.

Tristan Stone. Cf. CASTLE DORE and DRUSTANUS.

The Turk and Gawain. English rimed poem (c. 1500) in which GAWAIN beheads a challenger. The story has several points in common with the *Pèlerinage de Charlemagne*, which may be one of its sources.

Twrch Trwyth, Troit. In *Culhwch and Olwen*, the boar hunted by ARTHUR and his warriors. In order to marry OLWEN CULHWCH has to procure the razor, comb, and shears from the boar. He is mentioned in the *Gododdin*, is called

Troit in NENNIUS' *Mirabilia*, and finally becomes TORTAIN in the FIRST CONTINUATION of *Perceval*.

Tyolet. Anonymous twelfth-century Breton *lai* in which a maiden comes to ARTHUR'S court to find a knight to hunt a white stag. Tyolet succeeds, but, wounded by lions, he cannot return immediately, and is eventually found by GAWAIN.

U

Ulrich von Lichtenstein. In *Frauendienst*, gives an account of his adventures in the guise of KING ARTHUR in 1255.

Ulrich von Türheim. One of the continuations of GOTTFRIED'S *Tristan*.

Ulrich von Zatzikhoven. Cf. *Lanzelet*.

Urien. Sixth-century king of RHEGED, husband of MODRON and father of OWAIN. Both father and son are celebrated in TALIESIN'S poetry. He appears in the TRIADS though not in connection with ARTHUR. In *Claris et Laris*, he is father of YVAIN and Marine. Although the husband of MORGAN LE FAY in MALORY, he dies with ARTHUR fighting against MORDRED.

Uther Pendragon. In the *Dialogue with Glewlwyd Gafaelfawr*, mentioned as master of MABON and in the *Dialogue of Arthur and the Eagle* as father of Madog. (In Welsh *Uthr* means "terrible," *pen* "head chief," and *dragon*, "dragon," "leader.") In GEOFFREY he is the father of ARTHUR by means of an intrigue arranged by MERLIN and later dies of poison. In the Vulgate *Merlin* Uter, Son of Constant, becomes Uterpendragon when he succeeds his brother, Pendragon, to the throne. In the French versions and in MALORY, Uther is killed in battle.

V

Valliant, Jehan, de Poitiers. Compiled for Louis II, Duc de Bourbon, at the end of the fourteenth century a compendium of romances based on the history of England up to the collapse of ARTHUR's kingdom.

Vengeance Raguidel. Early thirteenth-century French romance by one Raoul. In this poem of 6182 lines written in the dialect of the Île de France, GAWAIN avenges the death of the knight Raguidel on his slayer, Guengasoain.

Verses on the Graves. Tenth-century BLACK BOOK verses (Poem XIX) recording the burial places of Welsh heroes. ARTHUR's grave is said to be "ANOETH," either "wonderful" or "unknown."

Vespasian. In the GRAIL tradition sets JOSEPH OF ARIMATHEA free.

Vita Columbae. Cf. ADOMNAN.

Vita Gildae. Cf. CARADOC OF LLANCARFAN.

Vita Merlini. GEOFFREY OF MONMOUTH's last work, c. 1149, a poem recounting the life and miraculous adventures of the seer whose prophecies he had earlier recorded in *Prophetiae Merlini.*

Viviane. Cf. LADY OF THE LAKE.

Voeux du Paon (The Vows of the Peacock). A late ALEXANDER THE GREAT romance (c. 1310) thought to be one of the sources of the English Alliterative *Morte Arthure.*

Vortigern. First appearing as Gwrtheyrn the Thin in the TRIADS (37, 51), he appears in GILDAS as the "proud king" who invited the Saxons to England. He comes to prominence in NENNIUS, however, where he attempts to build a tower on Mt. Snowdon as a defense against the Saxons. Told that he must sprinkle the ground with the blood of a child born without a father in order to stop the strange destruction which every night visits the site, he sends out his soldiers who discover the child AMBROSIUS who reveals that two sleeping dragons rest under the spot. In GEOFFREY the child AMBROSIUS is MERLIN who also prophesies the death of Vortigern. GEOFFREY also records that he became king through the murders of CONSTANTINE and his son CONSTANS and the exile of UTHER. He is eventually burned in his tower by UTHER.

Vortimer. The son of VORTIGERN.

Voyage of Bran. An eighth-century Irish account of BRAN's visit to the Underworld Island of Joy and Land of Women.

Vulgate Cycle (1215–1230). Thirteenth-century compilation of Old French prose romances of multiple, probably monastic, authorship. The first attempt to unify the vast body of Arthurian chronicles and romances, the Vulgate Cycle proper consists of three "original" loosely linked romances or "branches"—the prose *Lancelot*, the *Queste del Saint Graal*, and the *Mort Artu*—each of which represents the culmination of one of the three great lines of development within the Arthurian legend: the courtly, the religious, and the chronicle. To these branches were added two expansions of the original three, the *Estoire del Saint Graal*, a preliminary to the *Queste*, and the *Estoire de Merlin*, a preliminary to the *Mort Artu*. To these five romances is usually added as a part of the Vulgate Cycle the so-called Vulgate *Merlin*, actually a prose redaction of ROBERT DE BORON's *Merlin*, which does not survive in its complete poetic form. This prose *Merlin* is followed in the manuscripts of the Vulgate Cycle by a "historical" sequel and in the Huth manuscript by a "romantic" continuation generally called the *Suite du Merlin* which may be part of a "pseudo-ROBERT DE BORON cycle" of which the other branches do not survive except in such translations as the Portuguese *Demanda do Santo Graal*. However, the latest theorists maintain that the *Suite du Merlin* is part of a strongly GRAIL-oriented "post-Vulgate" cycle aptly called the *Roman du Graal*.

Vulgate Lancelot. Cf. *Lancelot.*
Vulgate Merlin. Cf. *Merlin.*
Vulgate Mort Artu. Cf. *Mort Artu.*

Wace. Norman poet (b. c. 1100), the author (1155) of a French verse paraphrase, the *Roman de Brut*, of GEOFFREY'S *Historia.* LAYAMON states that the *Brut* was written at the request of ELEANOR OF AQUITAINE, the wife of HENRY II of England. Wace's principal additions to GEOFFREY'S text, which he greatly enlarges, include an account of the creation of the ROUND TABLE, the presence of fairies at ARTHUR'S birth, and the legend of ARTHUR'S survival. His major contribution, however, lies in dramatizing and romanticizing GEOFFREY'S sober account and thus in pointing the way toward Arthurian romance.

Walwain, Walwanius, Walwanus, Walwen. Various Latin forms of GAWAIN.

Wartburgkrieg. Thirteenth-century German work which describes ARTHUR as living in a hollow mountain with hundreds of knights.

Wauchier de Denain. Thirteenth-century French writer to whom at one time were ascribed the first two continuations of CHRÉTIEN'S *Conte del Graal* which were once thought to be a single work. Recent scholarship, however, now regards both continuations to be anonymous even though the name of this writer of saints' lives is found in the SECOND CONTINUATION.

Wedding of Sir Gawain and Dame Ragnell. A mid-fifteenth-century romance utilizing the motif of the LOATHLY LADY TRANSFORMED. The story is that of Chaucer's *Wife of Bath's Tale*, though here the hag offers her husband a

choice of having her fair by day or by night, and she
later reveals that she had been made ugly by a step-
mother's spell. Both the construction and the verse of
the poem are inferior.

White Book of Rhydderch. A manuscript in the National Library of Wales at Aberystwyth containing, in Evans'
edition, the four "branches" of the *Mabinogion—Pwyll,
Branwen, Manawydan,* and *Math,—Peredur, The Dream of
Macsen, Lludd and Llefelys,* the *Dream of Rhonabwy,* the
Lady of the Fountain, Gereint, and *Culhwch and Olwen.* It
dates from 1300–25, some 75 years before the RED BOOK
OF HERGEST and may be its original, though both probably derive from a common source.

Wigalois. Early thirteenth-century German romance by Wirnt
von Gravenberg. The hero's adventures are similar to
those of GUINGLAIN though the poem contains more fantastic adventures—phantoms and enchantments and
even a Persian queen—than do the other BEL INCONNU
romances.

William of England. Cf. *Guillaume d'Angleterre.*

William of Malmesbury. Early twelfth-century Anglo-Norman
chronicler whose *Historia Regum Anglorum* (c. 1125) recounts in addition to information about ARTHUR derived
from NENNIUS the belief of the Bretons that ARTHUR will
return and that his grave is nowhere to be found. His
work *De Antiquitate Glastoniensis Ecclesiae* records that
ARTHUR was buried at GLASTONBURY and his body exhumed by the monks in 1190, but these statements are
probably interpolations of about 1250. William also suggests that the first missionaries to GLASTONBURY had
been sent from Gaul by St. Philip.

William of Newburgh. Late twelfth-century Anglo-Norman
chronicler notable as a critic of GEOFFREY OF MONMOUTH.

Winlogee. The form of GUINEVERE which appears on the MO-
DENA SCULPTURE.

Wisse, Claus, and Philipp Colin. Fourteenth-century Alsatian writers who expanded WOLFRAM's *Parzival* by means of translations of large portions of the French *Élucidation*.

Wolfram von Eschenbach. Bavarian knight of the early thirteenth century whose *Parzival* is one of the principal GRAIL romances. Written in the first decade of the thirteenth century, *Parzival* draws on a number of sources —principally CHRÉTIEN and the mysterious KYOT— though its themes, characterization, and emphasis are largely original. Its major contribution to the GRAIL legend and to Arthurian literature lies in its mystical conception of the GRAIL, not as the object of knightly adventure, but as a symbol of the unification of God and man, attainable only by God's chosen knight who, having lived the perfect earthly life, as a member of courtly society, asks the proper question at the GRAIL castle and himself becomes the GRAIL king. Wolfram is also the author of two incomplete works: the *Titurel*, based on an episode in CHRÉTIEN's *Perceval*, and the *Willehalm*, based on a *Chanson de Geste* of the William of Orange cycle.

Wooing of Emer. An early Irish saga, probably of the tenth century, relating the courtship of Emer, daughter of Forgall the Wily, by CUCHULAIN. One episode deals with DRUST and parallels the MORHOLT incident in the TRISTAN story.

Y

Yder. A secondary hero in *Vengeance Raguidel*. His life and fortunes are recounted in *Yder* where he assumes an importance greater than that of ARTHUR.

Yder. A French romance of 1210–25 dealing with the fortunes of the illegitimate Yder, who undertakes a series of adventures in order to win QUEEN GUENLOIE which includes defending a castle against ARTHUR, joining the ROUND

TABLE, and killing a bear and two giants. He is everywhere superior to the treacherous KAY and the jealous ARTHUR. Despite the fantastic nature of the adventures, the poem tends towards realism, especially in the scene (a possible source for *Sir Gawain and the Green Knight*) where Yder resists the advances of his host's wife by kicking her in the stomach.

Ymddiddan Myrddin a Thaliesin (The Dialogue of Myrddin and Taliesin). Welsh poem contained in the BLACK BOOK OF CARMARTHEN. The dialogue between seer and poet deals with (1) an attack made by one MAELGWN of GWYNEDD on DYFED in the first half of the sixth century and (2) the battle of ARFDERYDD.

Ynis Gutrin. Cf. AVALON.

Ynys Avallach. Early twelfth century name for GLASTONBURY. Cf. AVALON.

Ynys Wair. Cf. GWAIR.

Ynys Wydrin (Isle of Glass). The home of MELWAS. Cf. AVALON.

Ysbaddaden. Treacherous giant, father of OLWEN in *Culhwch and Olwen* whose eyes have to be propped open and who assigns a number of tasks, including the hunting of TWRCH TRWYTH, to the suitors of OLWEN. CULHWCH eventually performs the tasks and kills the giant.

Yvain. CHRÉTIEN's romance of the "Chevalier au Lion." The hero, having won LAUDINE, whose husband he has killed, forgets her during a year at ARTHUR's court and must undertake a series of adventures in order to regain his lady. The poem, composed after *Erec* and *Cligès* but possibly before *Lancelot*, deals as did *Erec*, with the conflict between the rival obligations of chivalry and marriage.

Yvain and Gawain. A fourteenth-century English redaction of CHRÉTIEN's *Yvain*. Successful as a poem in its own right, it replaces CHRÉTIEN's elegance with the homely and vigorous chivalry of the English style.